A Slave is a Slave • Piper, H. Beam

Publisher's Note

Purchase of this book entitles you to a free trial membership in the publisher's book club at www.rarebooksclub.com. (Time limited offer.) Simply enter the barcode number from the back cover onto the membership form on our home page. The book club entitles you to select from millions of books at no additional charge. You can also download a digital copy of this and related books to read on the go. Simply enter the title or subject onto the search form to find them.

Note: This is an historic book. Pages numbers, where present in the text, refer to the first edition of the book. The table of contents or index may also refer to them.

If you have any questions, could you please be so kind as to consult our Frequently Asked Questions page at www.rarebooksclub.com/faqs.cfm? You are also welcome to contact us there.

Publisher: General Books LLC™, Memphis, TN, USA, 2012. ISBN: 9781153756242.
Credits: Distributed Proofreaders.

❧ ❧ ❧ ❧ ❧ ❧ ❧ ❧

[Pg 62]

A SLAVE IS A SLAVE

BY H. BEAM PIPER

Transcriber's Note

This book was produced from Analog Science Fact—Science Fiction April 1962. Extensive research did not uncover any evidence that the U.S. copyright on this publication was renewed.

strong sympathy f

by cruel and overb

[Pg 63]

Jurgen, Prince Trevannion, accepted the coffee cup and lifted it to his lips, then lowered it. These Navy robots always poured coffee too hot; spacemen must have collapsium-lined throats. With the other hand, he punched a button on the robot's keyboard and received a lighted cigarette; turning, he placed the cup on the command-desk in front of him and looked about. The tension was relaxing in Battle-Control, the purposeful pandemonium of the last three hours dying rapidly. Officers of both sexes, in red and blue and yellow and green coveralls, were rising from seats, leaving their stations, gathering in groups. Laughter, a trifle loud; he realized, suddenly, that they had been worried, and wondered if he should not have been a little so himself. No. There would have been nothing he could have done about anything, so worry would not have been useful. He lifted the cup again and sipped cautiously.

"That's everything we can do now," the man beside him said. "Now we just sit and wait for the next move."

Like all the others, Line-Commodore Vann Shatrak wore shipboard battle-dress; his coveralls were black, splashed on breast and between shoulders with the gold insignia of his rank. His head was completely bald, and almost spherical; a beaklike nose carried down the curve of his brow, and the straight lines of mouth and chin chopped under it enhanced rather than spoiled the effect. He was getting coffee; he gulped it at once.

"It was very smart work, Commodore. I never saw a landing operation go so smoothly."

"Too smooth," Shatrak said. "I don't trust it." He looked suspiciously up at the row of viewscreens.

"It was absolutely unnecessary!"

That was young Obray, Count Erskyll, seated on the commodore's left. He was a generation younger than Prince Trevannion, as Shatrak was a generation older; they were both smooth-faced. It was odd, how beards went in and out of fashion with alternate generations. He had been worried, too, during the landing, but for a different reason from the others. Now he was reacting with anger.

"I told you, from the first, that it was unnecessary. You see? They weren't even able to defend themselves, let alone."

His personal communication-screen buzzed; he set down the coffee and flicked the switch. It was Lanze Degbrend. On the books, Lanze was carried as Assistant to the Ministerial Secretary. In practice, Lanze was his chess-opponent, conversational foil, right hand, third eye and ear, and, sometimes, trigger-finger. Lanze was now wearing the combat coveralls of an officer of Navy Landing-Troops; he had a steel helmet with a transpex visor shoved up, and there was a carbine slung over his shoulder. He grinned and executed an exaggeratedly military salute. He chuckled.

"Well, look at you; aren't you the perfect picture of correct diplomatic dress?"

"You know, sir, I'm afraid I am, for this planet," Degbrend said. "Colonel Ravney insisted on it. He says the situation downstairs is still fluid, which I take to mean that everybody is shooting at everybody. He says he has the main telecast station, in the big building the locals call the Citadel."

"Oh, good. Get our announcement out as quickly as you can. Number Five. You and Colonel Ravney can decide what interpolations are needed to fit the situation."

"Number Five; the really tough one," Degbrend considered. "I take it that by interpolations you do not mean dilutions?"

"Oh, no; don't water the drink. Spike it."

Lanze Degbrend grinned at him. Then he snapped down the visor of his helmet, unslung his carbine, and presented it. He was still standing at present arms when Trevannion blanked the screen.

"That still doesn't excuse a wanton and unprovoked aggression!" Erskyll was telling Shatrak, his thin face flushed and his voice quivering with indignation. "We came here to help these people, not to murder them."

"We didn't come here to do either, Obray," he said, turning to face the younger man. "We came here to annex their planet to the Galactic Empire, whether they wish it annexed or not. Commodore Shatrak used the quickest and most effective method of doing that. It would have done no good to attempt to parley with them from off-planet. You heard those telecasts of theirs."

"Authoritarian," Shatrak said, then mimicked pompously: "'Everybody is commanded to remain calm; the Mastership is taking action. The Convocation of the Lords-Master is in special session; they will decide how to deal with the invaders. The administrators are directed to reassure the supervisors; the overseers will keep the workers at their tasks. Any person disobeying the orders of the Mastership will be dealt with most severely.'"

"Static, too. No spaceships into this system for the last five hundred years; the Convocation—equals Parliament, I assume—hasn't been in special session for two hundred and fifty."

"Yes. I've taken over planets with that kind of government before," Shatrak said. "You can't argue with them. You just grab them by the center of authority, quick and hard."

Count Erskyll said nothing for a moment. He was opposed to the use of force. Force, he believed, was the last resort of incompetence; he had said so frequently enough since this operation had begun. Of course, he was absolutely right, though not in the way he meant. Only the incompetent wait until the last extremity to use force, and by then, it is usually too late to use anything, even prayer.

But, at the same time, he was opposed to authoritarianism, except, of course, when necessary for the real good of the people. And he did not like rulers who called themselves Lords-Master. Good democratic rulers called themselves Servants of the People. So he relapsed into silence and stared at the viewscreens.

One, from an outside pickup on the *Empress Eulalie* herself, showed the surface of the planet, a hundred miles down, the continent under them curving away to a distant sun-reflecting sea; beyond the curved horizon, the black sky was spangled with unwinking stars. Fifty miles down, the sun glinted from the three thousand foot globes of the two transport-cruisers, *Canopus* and *Mizar*.

Another screen, from *Mizar*, gave a clearer if more circumscribed view of the surface—green countryside, veined by rivers and wrinkled with mountains; little towns that were mere dots; a scatter of white clouds. Nothing that looked like roads. There had been no native sapient race on this planet, and in the thirteen centuries since it had been colonized the Terro-human population had never completely lost the use of contragravity vehicles. In that screen, farther down, the four destroyers, *Irma*, *Irene*, *Isobel* and *Iris*, were tiny twinkles.

From *Irene*, they had a magnified view of the city. On the maps, none later than eight hundred years old, it was called Zeggensburg; it had been built at the time of the first colonization under the old Terran Federation. Tall buildings, rising from wide interspaces of lawns and parks and gardens, and, at the very center, widely separated from anything else, the mass of the Citadel, a huge cylindrical tower rising from a cluster of smaller cylinders, with a broad circular landing stage above, topped by the newly raised flag of the Galactic Empire.

There was a second city, a thick crescent, to the south and east. The old maps placed the Zeggensburg spaceport there, but not a trace of that remained. In its place was what was evidently an industrial district, located where the prevailing winds would carry away the dust and smoke. There was quite a bit of both, but the surprising thing was the streets, long curved ones, and shorter ones crossing at regular intervals to form blocks. He had never seen a city with streets before, and he doubted if anybody else on the Empire ships had. Long boulevards to give unobstructed passage to low-level air-traffic, of course, and short winding walkways, but not things like these. Pictures, of course, of native cities on planets colonized at the time of the Federation, and even very ancient ones of cities on pre-Atomic Terra. But these people had contragravity; the towering, wide-spaced city beside this cross-gridded anachronism proved that.

They knew so little about this planet which they had come to bring under Imperial rule. It had been colonized thirteen centuries ago, during the last burst of expansion before the System States War and the disintegration of the Terran Federation, and it had been named Aditya, in the fashion of the times, for some forgotten deity of some obscure and ancient polytheism. A century or so later, it had seceded from or been abandoned by the Federation, then breaking up. That much they had gleaned from old [Pg 66] Federation records still existing on Baldur. After that, darkness, lighted only by a brief flicker when more records had turned up on Morglay.

Morglay was one of the Sword-Worlds, settled by refugee rebels from the System States planets. Mostly they had been soldiers and spacemen; there had been many women with them, and many were skilled technicians, engineers, scientists. They had managed to carry off considerable equipment with them, and for three centuries they had lived in isolation, spreading over a dozen hitherto undiscovered planets. Excalibur, Tizona, Gram, Morglay, Durendal, Flamberge, Curtana, Quernbiter; the names were a roll-call of fabulous blades of Old Terran legend.

Then they had erupted, suddenly and calamitously, into what was left of the Terran Federation as the Space Vikings, carrying pillage and destruction, until the newborn Empire rose to vanquish them. In the sixth Century Pre-Empire, one of their fleets had come from Morglay to Aditya.

The Adityans of that time had been near-barbarians; the descendants of the original settlers had been serfs of other barbarians who had come as mercenaries in the service of one or another of the local chieftains and had remained to loot and rule. Subjugating them had been easy; the Space Vikings had taken Aditya and made it their home. For several centuries, there had been communication between them and their home planet. Then Morglay had become involved in one of the interplanetary dynastic wars that had begun the decadence of the Space Vikings, and again Aditya dropped out of history.

Until this morning, when history returned in the black ships of the Galactic Empire.

He stubbed out the cigarette and summoned the robot to give him another. Shatrak was speaking:

"You see, Count Erskyll, we really had to do it this way, for their own good." He wouldn't have credited the commodore with such guile; anything was justified, according to Obray of Erskyll, if done for somebody else's good. "What we did, we just landed suddenly, knocked out their army, seized the center of government, before anybody could do anything. If we'd landed the way you'd wanted us to, somebody would have resisted, and the next thing, we'd have had to kill about five or six thousand of them and blow down a couple of towns, and we'd have lost a lot of our own people doing it. You might say, we had to do it to save them from themselves."

Obray of Erskyll seemed to have doubts, but before he could articulate them, Shatrak's communication-screen was calling attention to itself. The commodore flicked the switch, and his executive officer, Captain Patrique Morvill, appeared in it.

"We've just gotten reports, sir, that some of Ravney's people have captured a half-dozen missile-launching sites around the city. His air-reconn tells him that that's the lot of them. I have an officer of one of the parties that participated. You ought [Pg 67] to hear what he has to say, sir."

"Well, good!" Vann Shatrak whooshed out his breath. "I don't mind admitting, I was a little on edge about that."

"Wait till you hear what Lieutenant Carmath has to say." Morvill seemed to be strangling a laugh. "Ready for him, Commodore?"

Shatrak nodded; Morvill made a hand-signal and vanished in a flicker of rainbow colors; when the screen cleared, a young Landing-Troop lieutenant in battle-dress was looking out of it. He saluted and gave his name, rank and unit.

"This missile-launching site I'm occupying, sir; it's twenty miles northwest of the city. We took it thirty minutes ago; no resistance whatever. There are four hundred or so people here. Of them, twelve, one dozen, are soldiers. The rest are civilians. Ten enlisted men, a non-com of some sort, and something that appears to be an officer. The officer had a pistol, fully loaded. The non-com had a submachine gun, empty, with two loaded clips on his belt. The privates had rifles, empty, and no ammunition. The officer did not know where the rifle ammunition was stored."

Shatrak swore. The second lieutenant nodded. "Exactly my comment when he told me, sir. But this place is beautifully kept up. Lawns all mowed, trees neatly pruned, everything policed up like inspection morning. And there is a headquarters office building here adequate for an army division."

"How about the armament, Lieutenant?" Shatrak asked with forced patience.

"Ah, yes; the armament, sir. There are eight big launching cradles for pan-planetary or off-planet missiles. They are all polished up like the Crown Jewels. But none, repeat none, of them is operative. And there is not a single missile on the installation."

Shatrak's facial control didn't slip. It merely intensified, which amounted to the same thing.

"Lieutenant Carmath, I am morally certain I heard you correctly, but let's just check. You said."

He repeated the lieutenant back, almost word for word. Carmath nodded.

"That was it, sir. The missile-crypts are stacked full of old photoprints and recording and microfilm spools. The sighting-and-guidance systems for all the launchers are completely missing. The letoff mechanisms all lack major parts. There is an elaborate set of detection equipment, which will detect absolutely nothing. I saw a few pairs of binoculars about; I suspect that that is what we were first observed with."

"This office, now; I suppose all the paperwork is up to the minute in quintulplicate, and initialed by everybody within sight or hearing?"

"I haven't checked on that yet, sir. If you're thinking of betting on it, please don't expect me to cover you, though."

"Well, thank you, Lieutenant Carmath. Stick around; I'm sending down a tech-intelligence crew to look [Pg 68] at what's left of the place. While you're waiting, you might sort out whoever seems to be in charge and find out just what in Niffleheim he thinks that launching-station was maintained for."

"I think I can tell you that, now, Commodore," Prince Trevannion said as Shatrak blanked the screen. "We have a petrified authoritarianism. Quite likely some sort of an oligarchy; I'd guess that this Convocation thing they talk about consists of all the ruling class, everybody has equal voice, and nobody will take the responsibility for doing anything. And the actual work of government is [Pg 69] probably handled by a corps of bureaucrats entrenched in their jobs, unwilling to exert any effort and afraid to invite any criticism, and living only to retire on their pensions. I've seen governments like that before." He named a few. "One thing; once a government like that has been bludgeoned into the Empire, [Pg 70] it rarely makes any trouble later."

"Just to judge by this missileless nonlaunching station," Shatrak said, "they couldn't even decide on what kind of trouble to make, or how to start it. I think you're going to have a nice easy Proconsulate here, Count Erskyll."

Count Erskyll started to say something. No doubt he was about to tell Shatrak, cuttingly, that he didn't want an easy Proconsulate, but an opportunity to help these people. He was saved from this by the buzzing of Shatrak's communication-screen.

It was Colonel Pyairr Ravney, the Navy Landing-Troop commander. Like everybody else who had gone down to Zeggensburg, he was in battle-dress and armed; the transpex visor of his helmet was pushed up. Between Shatrak's generation and Count Erskyll's, he sported a pointed mustache and a spiky chin-beard, which, on his thin and dark-eyed face, looked distinctly Mephistophelean. He was grinning.

"Well, sir, I think we can call it a done job," he said. "There's a delegation here who want to talk to the Lords-Master of the ships on behalf of the Lords-Master of the Convocation. Two of them, with about a dozen portfolio-bearers and note-takers. I'm not too good in Lingua Terra, outside Basic, at best, and their brand is far from that. I gather that they're some kind of civil-servants, personal representatives of the top Lords-Master."

"Do we want to talk to them?" Shatrak asked.

"Well, we should only talk to the actual, titular, heads of the government—Mastership," Erskyll, suddenly protocol-conscious, objected. "We can't negotiate with subordinates."

"Oh, who's talking about negotiating; there isn't anything to negotiate. Aditya is now a part of the Galactic Empire. If this present regime assents to that, they can stay in power. If not, we will toss them out and install a new government. We will receive this delegation, inform them to that effect, and send them back to relay the information to their Lords-Master." He turned to the Commodore. "May I speak to Colonel Ravney?"

Shatrak assented. He asked Ravney where these Lords-Master were.

"Here in the Citadel, in what they call the Convocation Chamber. Close to a thousand of them, screaming recriminations at one another. Sounds like feeding time at the Imperial Zoo. I think they all want to surrender, but nobody dares propose it first. I've just put a cordon around it and placed it off limits to everybody. And everything outside off limits to the Convocation."

"Well thought of, Colonel. I suppose the Citadel teems with bureaucrats and such low life-forms?"

"Bulging with them. Literally thousands. Lanze Degbrend and Commander Douvrin and a few others are trying to get some sensible answers out of some of them."

"This delegation; how had you thought of sending them up?"

"Landing-craft to *Isobel*; *Isobel* [Pg 71] will bring them the rest of the way."

He looked at his watch. "Well, don't be in too much of a rush to get them here, Colonel. We don't want them till after lunch. Delay them on *Isobel*; the skipper can see that they have their own lunch aboard. And entertain them with some educational films. Something to convince them that there is slightly more to the Empire than one ship-of-the-line, two cruisers and four destroyers."

Count Erskyll was dissatisfied about that, too. He wanted to see the delegation at once and make arrangements to talk to their superiors. Count Erskyll, among other things, was zealous, and of this he disapproved. Zealous statesmen perhaps did more mischief than anything in the Galaxy—with the possible exception of procrastinating soldiers. That could indicate the fundamental difference between statecraft and war. He'd have to play with that idea a little. An Empire ship-of-the-line was almost a mile in diameter. It was more than a battle-craft; it also had political functions. The grand salon, on the outer zone where the curvature of the floors was less disconcerting, was as magnificent as any but a few of the rooms of the Imperial Palace at Asgard on Odin, the floor richly carpeted and the walls alternating mirrors and paintings. The movable furniture varied according to occasion; at present, it consisted of the bare desk at which they sat, the three chairs they occupied, and the three secretary-robots, their rectangular black casts blazened with the Sun and Cogwheel of the Empire. It faced the door, at the far end of the room; on either side, a rank of spacemen, in dress uniform and under arms, stood.

In principle, annexing a planet to the Empire was simplicity itself, but like so many things simple in principle, it was apt to be complicated in practice, and to this, he suspected, the present instance would be no exception.

In principle, one simply informed the planetary government that it was now subject to the sovereignty of his Imperial Majesty, the Galactic Emperor. This information was always conveyed by a Ministerial Secretary, directly under the Prime Minister and only one more step down from the Emperor, in the present instance Jurgen, Prince Trevannion. To make sure that the announcement carried conviction, the presumedly glad tidings were accompanied by the Imperial Space Navy, at present represented by Commodore Vann Shatrak and a seven ship battle-line unit, and two thousand Imperial Landing-Troops.

When the locals had been properly convinced—with as little bloodshed as necessary, but always beyond any dispute—an Imperial Proconsul, in this case Obray, Count Erskyll, would be installed. He would by no means govern the planet. The Imperial Constitution was definite on that point; every planetary government should be sovereign as to intraplanetary affairs. The Proconsul, within certain narrow and entirely inelastic limits, [Pg 72] would merely govern the government.

Unfortunately, Obray, Count Erskyll, appeared not to understand this completely. It was his impression that he was a torch-bearer of Imperial civilization, or something equally picturesque and metaphorical. As he conceived it, it was the duty of the Empire, as represented by himself, to make over backward planets like Aditya in the image of Odin or Marduk or Osiris or Baldur or, preferably, his own home world of Aton.

This was Obray of Erskyll's first proconsular appointment, it was due to family influence, and it was a mistake. Mistakes, of course, were inevitable in anything as large and complex as the Galactic Empire, and any institution guided by men was subject to one kind of influence or another, family influence being no worse than any other kind. In this case, the ultra-conservative Erskylls of Aton, from old Errol, Duke of Yorvoy, down, had become alarmed at the political radicalism of young Obray, and had, on his graduation from the University of Nefertiti, persuaded the Prime Minister to appoint him to a Proconsulate as far from Aton as possible, where he would not embarrass them. Just at that time, more important matters having been gotten out of the way, Aditya had come up for annexation, and Obray of Erskyll had been named Proconsul.

That had been the mistake. He should have been sent to some planet which had been under Imperial rule for some time, where the Proconsulate ran itself in a well-worn groove, and where he could at leisure learn the procedures and unlearn some of the unrealisms absorbed at the University from professors too well insulated from the realities of politics.

There was a stir among the guards; helmet-visors were being snapped down; feet scuffed. They stiffened to attention, the great doors at the other end of the grand salon slid open, and the guards presented arms as the Adityan delegation was ushered in.

There were fourteen of them. They all wore ankle-length gowns, and they all had shaven heads. The one in the lead carried a staff and wore a pale green gown; he was apparently a herald. Behind him came two in white gowns, their empty hands folded on their breasts; one was a huge bulk of obesity with a bulging brow, protuberant eyes and a pursey little mouth, and the other was thin and cadaverous, with a skull-like, almost fleshless face. The ones behind, in dark green and pale blue, carried portfolios and slung sound-recorder cases. There was a metallic twinkle at each throat; as they approached, he could see that they all wore large silver gorgets. They came to a halt twenty feet from the desk. The herald raised his staff.

"I present the Admirable and Trusty Tchall Hozhet, personal chief-slave of the Lord-Master Olvir Nikkolon, Chairman of the Presidium of the Lords-Master's Convocation, and Khreggor Chmidd, chief-slave in office to the Lord-Master Rovard Javasan, [Pg 73] Chief of Administration of Management of the Mastership," he said. Then he stopped, puzzled, looking from one to another of them. When his eyes fell on Vann Shatrak, he brightened.

"Are you," he asked, "the chief-slave of the chief Lord-Master of this ship?"

Shatrak's face turned pink; the pink darkened to red. He used a word; it was a completely unprintable word. So, except for a few scattered pronouns, conjunctions and prepositions, were the next fifty words he used. The herald stiffened. The two delegates behind him were aghast. The subordinate burden-bearers in the rear began looking around apprehensively.

"I," Shatrak finally managed, "am an officer of his Imperial Majesty's Space Navy. I am in command of this battle-line unit. I am *not*"—he reverted briefly to obscenity—"a slave."

"You mean, you are a Lord-Master, too?" That seemed to horrify the herald even more that the things Shatrak had been calling him. "Forgive me, Lord-Master. I did not think."

"That's right; you didn't," Shatrak agreed. "And don't call me Lord-Master again, or I'll."

"Just a moment, Commodore." He waved the herald aside and addressed the two in white gowns, shifting to Lingua Terra. "This is a ship of the Galactic Empire," he told them. "In the Empire, there are no slaves. Can you understand that?"

Evidently not. The huge one, Khreggor Chmidd, turned to the skull-faced Tchall Hozhet, saying: "Then they must all be Lords-Master." He saw the objection to that at once. "But how can one be a Lord-Master if there are no slaves?"

The horror was not all on the visitors' side of the desk, either. Obray of Erskyll was staring at the delegation and saying,

"Slaves!" under his breath. Obray of Erskyll had never, in his not-too-long life, seen a slave before.

"They can't be," Tchall Hozhet replied. "A Lord-Master is one who owns slaves." He gave that a moment's consideration. "But if they aren't Lords-Master, they must be slaves, and." No. That wouldn't do, either. "But a slave is one who belongs to a Lord-Master."

Rule of the Excluded Third; evidently Pre-Atomic formal logic had crept back to Aditya. Chmidd, looking around, saw the ranks of spacemen on either side, now at parade-rest.

"But aren't they slaves?" he asked.

"They are spacemen of the Imperial Navy," Shatrak roared. "Call one a slave to his face and you'll get a rifle-butt in yours. And I shan't lift a finger to stop it." He glared at Chmidd and Hozhet. "Who had the infernal impudence to send slaves to deal with the Empire? He needs to be taught a lesson."

"Why, I was sent by the Lord-Master Olvir Nikkolon, and."

"Tchall!" Chmidd hissed at him. "We cannot speak to Lords-Master. [Pg 74] We must speak to their chief-slaves."

"But they have no slaves," Hozhet objected. "Didn't you hear the . the one with the small beard . say so?"

"But that's ridiculous, Khreggor. Who does the work, and who tells them what to do? Who told these people to come here?"

"Our Emperor sent us. That is his picture, behind me. But we are not his slaves. He is merely the chief man among us. Do your Masters not have one among them who is chief?"

"That's right," Chmidd said to Hozhet. "In the Convocation, your Lord-Master is chief, and in the Mastership, my Lord-Master, Rovard Javasan, is chief."

"But they don't tell the other Lords-Master what to do. In Convocation, the other Lords-Master tell them."

"That's what I meant about an oligarchy," he whispered, in Imperial, to Erskyll.

"Suppose we tell Ravney to herd these Lords-Master onto a couple of landing-craft and bring them up here?" Shatrak suggested. He made the suggestion in Lingua Terra Basic, and loudly.

"I think we can manage without that." He raised his voice, speaking in Lingua Terra Basic:

"It does not matter whether these slaves talk to us or not. This planet is now under the rule of his Imperial Majesty, Rodrik III. If this Mastership wants to govern the planet under the Emperor, they may do so. If not, we will make an end of them and set up a new government here."

He paused. Chmidd and Hozhet were looking at one another in shocked incredulity.

"Tchall, they mean it," Chmidd said. "They can do it, too."

"We have nothing more to say to you slaves," he continued. "Hereafter, we will speak directly to the Lords-Master."

"But. The Lords-Master never do business directly," Hozhet said. "It is un-Masterly. Such discussions are between chief-slaves."

"This thing they call the Convocation," Shatrak mentioned. "I wonder if the members have the business done entirely through their slaves."

"Oh, no!" That shocked Chmidd into direct address. "No slave is allowed in the Convocation Chamber."

He wondered how they kept the place swept out. Robots, no doubt. Or else, what happened when the Masters weren't there didn't count.

"Very well. Your people have recorders; are they on?"

Hozhet asked Chmidd; Chmidd asked the herald, who asked one of the menials in the rear, who asked somebody else. The reply came back through the same channels; they were.

"Very well. At this time tomorrow, we will speak to the Convocation of Lords-Master. Commodore Shatrak, see to it that Colonel Ravney has them in the Convocation Chamber, and that preparations in the room are made, so that we may address them in the dignity befitting representatives of his Imperial Majesty." [Pg 75] He turned to the Adityan slaves. "That is all. You have permission to go."

They watched the delegation back out, with the honor-guard following. When the doors had closed behind them, Shatrak ran his hand over his bald head and laughed.

"Shaved heads, every one of them. That's probably why they thought I was your slave. Bet those gorgets are servile badges, too." He touched the Knight's Star of the Order of the Empire at his throat. "Probably thought that was what this was. We would have to draw something like this!"

"They simply can't imagine anybody not being either a slave or a slave-owner," Erskyll was saying. "That must mean that there is no free non-slave-holding class at all. Universal slavery! Well, we'll have to do something about that. Proclaim total emancipation, immediately."

"Oh, no; we can't do anything like that. The Constitution won't permit us to. Section Two, Article One: *Every Empire planet shall be self-governed as to its own affairs, in the manner of its own choice, and without interference.*"

"But slavery. Section Two, Article Six," Erskyll objected. "*There shall be no chattel slavery or serfdom anywhere in the Empire; no sapient being of any race whatsoever shall be the property of any being but himself.*"

"That's correct," he agreed. "If this Mastership intends to remain the planetary government under the Empire, they will be obliged to abolish slavery, but they will have to do it by their own act. We cannot do it for them."

"You know what I'd do, Prince Trevannion?" Shatrak said. "I'd just heave this Mastership thing out, and set up a nice tight military dictatorship. We have the planet under martial rule now; let's just keep it that way for about five years, till we can train a new government."

That suggestion seemed to pain Count Erskyll almost as much as the existing situation.

They dined late, in Commodore Shatrak's private dining room. Beside Shatrak, Erskyll and himself, there were Lanze Degbrend, and Count Erskyll's charge-d'affaires, Sharll Ernanday, and

Patrique Morvill and Pyairr Ravney and the naval intelligence officer, Commander Andrey Douvrin. Ordinarily, he deplored serious discussion at meals, but under the circumstances it was unavoidable; nobody could think or talk of anything else. The discussion which he had hoped would follow the meal began before the soup-course.

"We have a total population of about twenty million," Lanze Degbrend reported. "A trifle over ten thousand Masters, all ages and both sexes. The remainder are all slaves."

"I find that incredible," Erskyll declared promptly. "Twenty million people, held in slavery by ten thousand! Why do they stand for it? Why don't they rebel?"

"Well, I can think of three good [Pg 76] reasons," Douvrin said. "Three square meals a day."

"And no responsibilities; no need to make decisions," Degbrend added. "They've been slaves for seven and a half centuries. They don't even know the meaning of freedom, and it would frighten them if they did."

"Chain of command," Shatrak said. When that seemed not to convey any meaning to Erskyll, he elaborated: "We have a lot of dirty-necked working slaves. Over every dozen of them is an overseer with a big whip and a stungun. Over every couple of overseers there is a guard with a submachine gun. Over them is a supervisor, who doesn't need a gun because he can grab a handphone and call for troops. Over the supervisors, there are higher supervisors. Everybody has it just enough better than the level below him that he's afraid of losing his job and being busted back to fieldhand."

"That's it exactly, Commodore," Degbrend said. "The whole society is a slave hierarchy. Everybody curries favor with the echelon above, and keeps his eye on the echelon below to make sure he isn't being undercut. We have something not too unlike that, ourselves. Any organizational society is, in some ways, like a slave society. And everything is determined by established routine. The whole thing has simply been running on momentum for at least five centuries, and if we hadn't come smashing in with a situation none of the routines covered, it would have kept on running for another five, till everything [Pg 77] wore out and stopped. I heard about those missile-stations, by the way. They're typical of everything here."

"That's another thing," Erskyll interrupted. "These Lords-Master are the descendants of the old Space-Vikings, and the slaves of the original inhabitants. The Space Vikings were a technologically advanced people; they had all the old Terran Federation science and technology, and a lot they developed for themselves on the Sword-Worlds."

"Well? They still had a lot of it, on the Sword-Worlds, two centuries ago when we took them over."

"But technology always drives out slavery; that's a fundamental law of socio-economics. Slavery is economically unsound; it cannot compete with power-industry, let alone cybernetics and robotics."

He was tempted to remind young Obray of Erskyll that there were no such things as fundamental laws of socio-economics; merely usually reliable generalized statements of what can more or less be depended upon to happen under most circumstances. He resisted the temptation. Count Erskyll had had enough shocks, today, without adding to them by gratuitous blasphemy.

"In this case, Obray, it worked in reverse. The Space Vikings enslaved the Adityans to hold them in subjugation. That was a politico-military necessity. Then, being committed to slavery, with a slave population who had to be made to earn their keep, they found cybernetics and robotics economically unsound."

"And almost at once, they began appointing slave overseers, and the technicians would begin training slave assistants. Then there would be slave supervisors to direct the overseers, slave administrators to direct them, slave secretaries and bookkeepers, slave technicians and engineers."

"How about the professions, Lanze?"

"All slave. Slave physicians, teachers, everything like that. All the Masters are taught by slaves; the slaves are educated by apprenticeship. The courts are in the hands of slaves; cases are heard by the chief slaves of judges who don't even know where their own courtrooms are; every Master has a team of slave lawyers. Most of the lawsuits are estate-inheritance cases; some of them have been in litigation for generations."

"What do the Lords-Master do?" Shatrak asked.

"Masterly things," Degbrend replied. "I was only down there since noon, but from what I could find out, that consists of feasting, making love to each other's wives, being entertained by slave performers, and feuding for social precedence like wealthy old ladies on Odin."

"You got this from the slaves? How did you get them to talk, Lanze?"

Degbrend and Ravney exchanged amused glances. Ravney said:

"Well, I detailed a sergeant and six privates to accompany Honorable Degbrend," Ravney said. "They. How would you put it, Lanze?" [Pg 78]

"I asked a slave a question. If he refused to answer, somebody knocked him down with a rifle-butt," Degbrend replied. "I never had to do that more than once in any group, and I only had to do it three times in all. After that, when I asked questions, I was answered promptly and fully. It is surprising how rapidly news gets around the Citadel."

"You mean you had those poor slaves beaten?" Erskyll demanded.

"Oh, no. Beating implies repeated blows. We only gave one to a customer; that was enough."

"Well, how about the army, if that's what those people in the long red-brown coats were?" Shatrak changed the subject by asking Ravney.

"All slave, of course, officers and all.

What will we do about them, sir? I have about three thousand, either confined to their barracks or penned up in the Citadel. I requisitioned food for them, paid for it in chits. There were a few isolated companies and platoons that gave us something of a fight; most of them just threw away their weapons and bawled for quarter. I've segregated the former; with your approval, I'll put them under Imperial officers and noncoms for a quickie training in our tactics, and then use them to train the rest."

"Do that, Pyairr. We only have two thousand men of our own, and that's not enough. Do you think you can make soldiers out of any of them?"

"Yes, I believe so, sir. They are trained, organized and armed for civil-order work, which is what we'll need them for ourselves. In the entire history of this army, all they have done has been to overawe unarmed slaves; I am sure they have never been in combat with regular troops. They have an elaborate set of training and field regulations for the sort of work for which they were intended. What they encountered today was entirely outside those regulations, which is why they behaved as they did."

"Did you have any trouble getting cooperation from the native officers?" Shatrak asked.

"Not in the least. They cooperated quite willingly, if not always too intelligently. I simply told them that they were now the personal property of his Imperial Majesty, Rodrik III. They were quite flattered by the change of ownership. If ordered to, I believe that they would fire on their former Lords-Master without hesitation."

"You told those slaves that they . belonged . to the *Emperor*?"

Count Erskyll was aghast. He stared at Ravney for an instant, then snatched up his brandy-glass—the meal had gotten to that point—and drained it at a gulp. The others watched solicitously while he coughed and spluttered over it.

"Commodore Shatrak," he said sternly. "I hope that you will take severe disciplinary action; this is the most outrageous."

"I'll do nothing of the sort," Shatrak [Pg 79] retorted. "The colonel is to be commended; did the best thing he could, under the circumstances. What are you going to do when slavery is abolished here, Colonel?"

"Oh, tell them that they have been given their freedom as a special reward for meritorious service, and then sign them up for a five year enlistment."

"That might work. Again, it might not."

"I think, Colonel, that before you do that, you had better disarm them again. You might possibly have some trouble, otherwise."

Ravney looked at him sharply. "They might not want to be free? I'd thought of that."

"Nonsense!" Erskyll declared. "Who ever heard of slaves rebelling against freedom?"

Freedom was a Good Thing. It was a Good Thing for everybody, everywhere and all the time. Count Erskyll knew it, because freedom was a Good Thing for him.

He thought, suddenly, of an old tomcat belonging to a lady of his acquaintance at Paris-on-Baldur, a most affectionate cat, who insisted on catching mice and bringing them as presents to all his human friends. To this cat's mind, it was inconceivable that anybody would not be most happy to receive a nice fresh-killed mouse.

"Too bad we have to set any of them free," Vann Shatrak said. "Too bad we can't just issue everybody new servile gorgets marked, *Personal Property of his Imperial Majesty* and let it go at that. But I guess we can't."

"Commodore Shatrak, you are joking," Erskyll began.

"I hope I am," Shatrak replied grimly. The top landing-stage of the Citadel grew and filled the forward viewscreen of the ship's launch. It was only when he realized that the tiny specks were people, and the larger, birdseed-sized, specks vehicles, that the real size of the thing was apparent. Obray of Erskyll, beside him, had been silent. He had been looking at the crescent-shaped industrial city, like a servile gorget around Zeggensburg's neck.

"The way they've been crowded together!" he said. "And the buildings; no space between. And all that smoke! They must be using fossil-fuel!"

"It's probably too hard to process fissionables in large quantities, with what they have."

"You were right, last evening. These people have deliberately halted progress, even retrogressed, rather than give up slavery."

Halting progress, to say nothing of retrogression, was an unthinkable crime to him. Like freedom, progress was a Good Thing, anywhere, at all times, and without regard to direction.

Colonel Ravney met them when they left the launch. The top landing-stage was swarming with Imperial troops.

"Convocation Chamber's three stages down," he said. "About two [Pg 80] thousand of them there now; been coming in all morning. We have everything set up." He laughed. "They tell me slaves are never permitted to enter it. Maybe, but they have the place bugged to the ceiling all around."

"Bugged? What with?" Shatrak asked, and Erskyll was wanting to know what he meant. No doubt he thought Ravney was talking about things crawling out of the woodwork.

"Screen pickups, radio pickups, wired microphones; you name it and it's there. I'll bet every slave in the Citadel knows everything that happens in there while it's happening."

Shatrak wanted to know if he had done anything about them. Ravney shook his head.

"If that's how they want to run a government, that's how they have a right to run it. Commander Douvrin put in a few of our own, a little better camouflaged than theirs."

There were more troops on the third stage down. They formed a procession down a long empty hallway, a few scared-looking slaves peeping from doorways at them. There were more troops where the corridor ended in great double doors, emblazoned with a straight broad-sword diagonally across an eight-pointed star. Emblematology of planets conquered by the Space Vikings always included swords and stars. An officer gave a signal; the doors started to slide apart, and within, from a screen-speaker, came a fanfare of trumpets.

At first, all he could see was the projection-screen, far ahead, and the <u>tessellated</u> aisle stretching toward it. The trumpets stopped, and they advanced, and then he saw the Lords-Master.

They were massed, standing among benches on either side, and if anything Pyairr Ravney had understated their numbers. They all wore black, trimmed with gold; he wondered if the coincidence that these were also the Imperial colors might be useful. Queer garments, tightly fitted tunics at the top which became flowing robes below the waist, deeply scalloped at the edges. The sleeves were exaggeratedly wide; a knife or a pistol, and not necessarily a small one, could be concealed in every one. He was sure that thought had entered Vann Shatrak's mind. They were armed, not with dress-daggers, but with swords; long, straight cross-hilted broadswords. They were the first actual swords he had ever seen, except in museums or on the stage.

There was a bench of gold and onyx at the front, where, normally the seven-man Presidium sat, and in front of it were thronelike seats for the Chiefs of Managements, equivalent to the Imperial Council of Ministers. Because of the projection screen that had been installed, they had all been moved to an improvised dais on the left. There was another dais on the right, under a canopy of black and gold velvet, emblazoned with the gold sun and superimposed black cogwheel of the Empire. There were three thrones, for himself, Shatrak, [Pg 81] and Erskyll, and a number of lesser but still imposing chairs for their staffs.

They took their seats. He slipped the earplug of his memophone into his left ear and pressed the stud in the middle of his Grand Star of the Order of Odin. The memophone began giving him the names of the Presidium and of the Chiefs of Managements. He wondered how many upper-slaves had been gun-butted to produce them.

"Lords and Gentlemen," he said, after he had greeted them and introduced himself and the others, "I speak to you in the name of his Imperial Majesty, Rodrik III. His Majesty will now greet you in his own voice, by recording."

He pressed a button on the arm of his chair. The screen lighted, flickered, and steadied, and the trumpets blared again. When the fanfare ended, a voice thundered:

"*The Emperor speaks!*"

Rodrik III compromised on the beard question with a small mustache. He wore the stern but kindly expression the best theatrical directors in Asgard had taught him; Public Face Number Three. He inclined his head slightly and stiffly, as a man wearing a seven-pound crown must.

"We greet our subjects of Aditya to the fellowship of the Empire. We have long had good reports of you, and we are happy now to speak to you. Deserve well of us, and prosper under the Sun and Cogwheel."

Another fanfare, as the image vanished. Before any of the Lords-Master could find voice, he was speaking to them:

"Well, Lords and Gentlemen, you have been welcomed into the Empire by his Majesty. I know, there hasn't been a ship in or out of this system for five centuries, and I suppose you have a great many questions to ask about the Galactic Empire. Members of the Presidium and Chiefs of Managements may address me directly; others will please address the chairman."

Olvir Nikkolon, the owner of Tchall Hozhet, was on his feet at once. He had a loose-lipped mouth and a not entirely straight nose and pale eyes that were never entirely still.

"What I want to know is; why did you people have to come here to take our planet away from us? Isn't the rest of the Galaxy big enough for you?"

"No, Lord Nikkolon. The Galaxy is not big enough for any competition of sovereignty. There must be one and only one completely sovereign power. The Terran Federation was once such a power. It failed, and vanished; you know what followed. Darkness and anarchy. We are clawing our way up out of that darkness. We will not fail. We will create a peaceful and unified Galaxy."

He talked to them, about the collapse of the old Federation, about the interstellar wars, about the Neobarbarians, about the long night. He told them how the Empire had risen on a few planets five thousand light-years [Pg 82] away, and how it had spread.

"We will not repeat the mistakes of the Terran Federation. We will not attempt to force every planetary government into a common pattern, or dictate the ways in which they govern themselves. We will foster in every way peaceful trade and communication. But we will not again permit the plague of competing sovereignties, the condition under which war is inevitable. The first attempt to set up such a sovereignty in competition with the Empire will be crushed mercilessly, and no planet inhabited by any sapient race will be permitted to remain outside the Empire.

"Lords and Gentlemen, permit me to show you a little of what we have already accomplished, in the past three hundred years."

He pressed another button. The screen flickered, and the show started. It lasted for almost two hours; he used a handphone to interject comments and explanations. He showed them planet after planet—Marduk, where the Empire had begun, Baldur, Vishnu, Belphegor, Morglay, whence their ancestors had come, Amaterasu, Irminsul, Fafnir, finally Odin, the Imperial Planet. He showed towering cities swarming with aircars; spaceports where the huge globes of interstellar ships landed and lifted out; farms and industries; vast crowds at public celebrations; troop-reviews and naval bases and fleet-maneuvers; historical views of the battles that had created Imperial power.

"That, Lords and Gentlemen, is what you have an opportunity to bring your planet into. If you accept, you will continue to rule Aditya under the Empire. If you refuse, you will only put us to the inconvenience of replacing you with a new planetary government, which will be annoying for us and, probably, fatal for you."

Nobody said anything for a few minutes. Then Rovard Javasan, the Chief of Administration and the owner of the mountainous Khreggor Chmidd, rose.

"Lords and Gentlemen, we cannot resist anything like this," he said. "We cannot even resist the force they have here; that was tried yesterday, and you all saw what happened. Now, Prince Trevannion; just to what extent will the Mastership retain its sovereignty under the Empire?"

"To practically the same extent as at present. You will, of course, acknowledge the Emperor as your supreme ruler, and will govern subject to the Imperial Constitution. Have you any colonies on any of the other planets of this system?"

"We had a shipyard and docks on the inner moon, and we had mines on the fourth planet of this system, but it is almost airless and the colony was limited to a couple of dome-cities. Both were abandoned years ago."

"Both will be reopened before long, I daresay. We'd better make the limits of your sovereignty the orbit of the outer planet of this system. You may have your own normal-space ships, but the Empire will control [Pg 113] all hyperdrive craft, and all nuclear weapons. I take it you are the sole government on this planet? Then no other will be permitted to compete with you."

"Well, what are they taking away from us, then?" somebody in the rear asked.

"I assume that you are agreed to accept the sovereignty of his Imperial Majesty? Good. As a matter of form, Lord Nikkolon, will you take a vote? His Imperial Majesty would be most gratified if it were unanimous."

Somebody insisted that the question would have to be debated, which meant that everybody would have to make a speech, all two thousand of them. He informed them that there was nothing to debate; they were confronted with an accomplished fact which they must accept. So Nikkolon made a speech, telling them at what a great moment in Adityan history they stood, and concluded by saying:

"I take it that it is the unanimous will of this Convocation that the sovereignty of the Galactic Emperor be acknowledged, and that we, the 'Mastership of Aditya' do here proclaim our loyal allegiance to his Imperial Majesty, Rodrik the Third. Any dissent? Then it is ordered so recorded."

Then he had to make another speech, to inform the representatives of his new sovereign of the fact. Prince Trevannion, in the name of the Emperor, delivered the well-worn [Pg 114] words of welcome, and Lanze Degbrend got the coronet out of the black velvet bag under his arm and the Imperial Proconsul, Obray, Count Erskyll, was crowned. Erskyll's charge-d'affaires, Sharll Ernanday, produced the scroll of the Imperial Constitution, and Erskyll began to read.

Section One: The universality of the Empire. The absolute powers of the Emperor. The rules of succession. The Emperor also to be Planetary King of Odin.

Section Two: Every planetary government to be sovereign in its own internal affairs. Only one sovereign government upon any planet, or within normal-space travel distance. All hyperspace ships, and all nuclear weapons. No planetary government shall make war . enter into any alliance . tax, regulate or restrain interstellar trade or communication. Every sapient being shall be equally protected.

Then he came to Article Six. He cleared his throat, raised his voice, and read:

"*There shall be no chattel-slavery or serfdom anywhere in the Empire; no sapient being, of any race whatsoever, shall be the property of any being but himself.*"

The Convocation Chamber was silent, like a bomb with a defective fuse, for all of thirty seconds. Then it blew up with a roar. Out of the corner of his eye, he saw the doors slide apart and an airjeep, bristling with machine guns, float in and rise to the ceiling. The first inarticulate roar was followed by a babel of voices, like a tropical cloudburst on a prefab hut. Olvir Nikkolon's mouth was working as he shouted unheard.

He pressed another of the row of buttons on the arm of his chair. Out of the screen-speaker a voice, as loud, by actual sound-meter test, as an anti-vehicle gun, thundered:

"SILENCE!"

Into the shocked stillness which it produced, he spoke, like a schoolmaster who has returned to find his room in an uproar:

"Lord Nikkolon; what is this nonsense? You are Chairman of the Presidium; is this how you keep order here? What is this, a planetary parliament or a spaceport saloon?"

"You tricked us!" Nikkolon accused. "You didn't tell us about that article when we voted. Why, our whole society is based on slavery!"

Other voices joined in:

"That's all right for you people, you have robots."

"Maybe you don't know it, but there are twenty million slaves on this planet."

"Look, you can't free slaves! That's ridiculous. A slave's a *slave*!"

"Who'll do the work? And who would they belong to? They'd have to belong to somebody!"

"What I want to know," Rovard Javasan made himself heard, is, "*how are you going to free them?*"

There was an ancient word, originating in one of the lost languages of Pre-Atomic Terra—*sixtifor*. It meant, the basic, fundamental, question. Rovard Javasan, he suspected, had just asked the sixtifor. Of course, Obray, [Pg 115] Count Erskyll, Planetary Proconsul of Aditya, didn't realize that. He didn't even know what Javasan meant. Just free them. Commodore Vann Shatrak couldn't see much of a problem, either.

He would have answered, Just free them, and then shoot down the first two or three thousand who took it seriously. Jurgen, Prince Trevannion, had no intention whatever of attempting to answer the sixtifor.

"My dear Lord Javasan, that is the problem of the Adityan Mastership. They are your slaves; we have neither the intention nor the right to free them. But let me remind you that slavery is specifically prohibited by the Imperial Constitution; if you do not abolish it immediately, the Empire will be forced to intervene. I believe, toward the last of those audio-visuals, you saw some examples of Imperial intervention."

They had. A few looked apprehensively at the ceiling, as though expecting the hellburners and planet-busters and nega-matter-bombs at any moment. Then one of the members among the benches rose.

"We don't know how we are going to do it, Prince Trevannion," he said. "We will do it, since this is the Empire law, but you will have to tell us how."

"Well, the first thing will have to be an Act of Convocation, outlawing the ownership of one being by another. Set some definite date on which the slaves must all be freed; that need not be too immediate. Then, I would suggest that you set up some agency to handle all the details. And, as soon as you have enacted the abolition of slavery, which should be this afternoon, appoint a committee, say a dozen of you, to confer with Count Erskyll and myself. Say you have your committee aboard the *Empress Eulalie* in six hours. We'll have transportation arranged by then. And let me point out, I hope for the last time, that we discuss matters directly, without intermediaries. We don't want any more slaves, pardon, freedmen, coming aboard to talk for you, as happened yesterday."

Obray, Count Erskyll, was unhappy about it. He did not think that the Lords-Master were to be trusted to abolish slavery; he said so, on the launch, returning to the ship. Jurgen, Prince Trevannion was inclined to agree. He doubted if any of the Lords-Master he had seen were to be trusted, unassisted, to fix a broken mouse-trap.

Line-Commodore Vann Shatrak was also worried. He was wondering how long it would take for Pyairr Ravney to make useful troops out of the newly-surrendered slave soldiers, and where he was going to find contragravity to shift them expeditiously from trouble-spot to trouble-spot. Erskyll thought he was anticipating resistance on the part of the Masters, and for once he approved the use of force. Ordinarily, force was a Bad Thing, but this was a Good Cause, which justified any means.

They entertained the committee from the Convocation for dinner, [Pg 116] that evening. They came aboard stiffly hostile—most understandably so, under the circumstances—and Prince Trevannion exerted all his copious charm to thaw them out, beginning with the pre-dinner cocktails and continuing through the meal. By the time they retired for coffee and brandy to the parlor where the conference was to be held, the Lords-ex-Masters were almost friendly.

"We've enacted the Emancipation Act," Olvir Nikkolon, who was ex officio chairman of the committee, reported. "Every slave on the planet must be free before the opening of the next Midyear Feasts."

"And when will that be?"

Aditya, he knew, had a three hundred and fifty-eight day year; even if the Midyear Feasts were just past, they were giving themselves very little time. In about a hundred and fifty days, Nikkolon said.

"Good heavens!" Erskyll began, indignantly.

"I should say so, myself," he put in, cutting off anything else the new Proconsul might have said. "You gentlemen are allowing yourselves dangerously little time. A hundred and fifty days will pass quite rapidly, and you have twenty million slaves to deal with. If you start at this moment and work continuously, you'll have a little under a second apiece for each slave."

The Lords-Master looked dismayed. So, he was happy to observe, did Count Erskyll.

"I assume you have some system of slave registration?" he continued.

That was safe. They had a bureaucracy, and bureaucracies tend to have registrations of practically everything.

"Oh, yes, of course," Rovard Javasan assured him. "That's your Management, isn't it, Sesar; Servile Affairs?"

"Yes, we have complete data on every slave on the planet," Sesar Martwynn, the Chief of Servile Management, said. "Of course, I'd have to ask Zhorzh about the details."

Zhorzh was Zhorzh Khouzhik, Martwynn's chief-slave in office.

"At least, he was my chief-slave; now you people have taken him away from me. I don't know what I'm going to do without him. For that matter, I don't know what poor Zhorzh will do, either."

"Have you gentlemen informed your chief-slaves that they are free, yet?"

Nikkolon and Javasan looked at each other. Sesar Martwynn laughed.

"They know," Javasan said. "I must say they are much disturbed."

"Well, reassure them, as soon as you're back at the Citadel," he told them. "Tell them that while they are now free, they need not leave you unless they so desire; that you will provide for them as before."

"You mean, we can keep our chief-slaves?" somebody cried.

"Yes, of course—chief-freedmen, you'll have to call them, now. You'll have to pay them a salary."

"You mean, give them money?" Ranal Valdry, the Lord Provost-Marshal demanded, incredulously. "Pay our own slaves?" [Pg 117]

"You idiot," somebody told him, "they aren't our slaves any more. That's the whole point of this discussion."

"But . but how can we pay slaves?" one of the committeemen-at-large asked. "Freedmen, I mean?"

"With money. You do have money, haven't you?"

"Of course we have. What do you think we are, savages?"

"What kind of money?"

Why, money; what did he think? The unit was the star-piece, the stelly. When he asked to see some of it, they were indignant. Nobody carried money; wasn't Masterly. A Master never even touched the stuff; that was what slaves were for. He wanted to know how it was secured, and they didn't know what he meant, and when he tried to explain their incomprehension deepened. It seemed that the Mastership issued money to finance itself, and individual Masters issued money on their personal credit, and it was handled through the Mastership Banks.

"That's Fedrig Daffysan's Management; he isn't here," Rovard Javasan said. "I can't explain it, myself."

And without his chief-slave, Fedrig Daffysan probably would not be able to, either.

"Yes, gentlemen. I understand. You have money. Now, the first thing you will have to do is furnish us with a complete list of all the slave-owners on the planet, and a list of all the slaves held by each. This will be sent back to Odin, and will be the basis for the compensation to be paid for the destruction of your property-rights in these slaves. How much is a slave worth, by the way?"

Nobody knew. Slaves were never sold; it wasn't Masterly to sell one's slaves. It wasn't even heard of.

"Well, we'll arrive at some valuation. Now, as soon as you get back to the Citadel, talk at once to your former chief-slaves, and their immediate subordinates, and explain the situation to them. This can be passed down through administrative freedmen to the workers; you must see to it that it is clearly understood, at all levels, that as long as the freedmen remain at their work they will be provided for and paid, but that if they quit your service they will receive nothing. Do you think you can do that?"

"You mean, give them everything we've been giving them now, and then pay them money?" Ranal Valdry almost howled.

"Oh, no. You pay them a fixed wage. You charge them for everything you give them, and deduct that from their wages. It will mean considerable extra bookkeeping, but outside of that I believe you'll find that things will go along much as they always did."

The Masters had begun to relax, and by the time he was finished all of them were smiling in relief. Count Erskyll, on the other hand, was almost writhing in his chair. It must be horrible to be a brilliant young Proconsul of liberal tendencies and to have to sit mute while a cynical old Ministerial Secretary, vastly one's superior [Pg 118] in the Imperial Establishment and a distant cousin of the Emperor to boot, calmly bartered away the sacred liberties of twenty million people.

"But would that be legal, under the Imperial Constitution?" Olvir Nikkolon asked.

"I shouldn't have suggested it if it hadn't been. The Constitution only forbids physical ownership of one sapient being by another; it emphatically does not guarantee anyone an unearned livelihood."

The Convocation committee returned to Zeggensburg to start preparing the servile population for freedom, or reasonable facsimile. The chief-slaves would take care of that; each one seemed to have a list of other chief-slaves, and the word would spread from them on an each-one-call-five system. The public announcement would be postponed until the word could be passed out to the upper servile levels. A meeting with the chief-slaves in office of the various Managements was scheduled for the next afternoon.

Count Erskyll chatted with forced affability while the departing committeemen were being seen to the launch that would take them down. When the airlock closed behind them, he drew Prince Trevannion aside out of earshot of their subordinates.

"You know what you're doing?" he raged, in a hoarse whisper. "You're simply substituting peonage for outright slavery!"

"I'd call that something of a step." He motioned Erskyll into one of the small hall-cars, climbed in beside him, and lifted it, starting toward the living-area. "The Convocation has acknowledged the principle that sapient beings should not be property. That's a great deal, for one day."

"But the people will remain in servitude, you know that. The Masters will keep them in debt, and they'll be treated just as brutally."

"Oh, there will be abuses; that's to be expected. This Freedmen's Management, nee Servile Management, will have to take care of that. Better make a memo to talk with this chief-freedman of Martwynn's, what's his name? Zhorzh Khouzhik; that's right, let Zhorzh do it. Employment Practices Code, investigation agency, enforcement. If he can't do the job, that's not our fault. The Empire does not guarantee every planet an honest, intelligent and efficient government; just a single one."

"But."

"It will take two or three generations. At first, the freedmen will be exploited just as they always have been, but in time there will be protests, and disorders, and each time, there will be some small improvement. A society must evolve, Obray. Let these people earn their freedom. Then they will be worthy of it."

"They should have their freedom now."

"This present generation? What do you think freedom means to them? *We don't have to work, any more.* So down tools and let everything stop at once. *We can do anything we want to.* Let's kill the overseer. [Pg 119] And: *Anything that belongs to the Masters belongs to us; we're Masters too, now.* No, I think it's better, for the present, to tell them that this freedom business is just a lot of Masterly funny-talk, and that things aren't really being changed at all. It will effect a considerable saving of his Imperial Majesty's ammunition, for one thing."

He dropped Erskyll at his apartment and sent the hall-car back from his own. Lanze Degbrend was waiting for him when he entered.

"Ravney's having trouble. That is the word he used," Degbrend said. In Pyairr Ravney's lexicon, trouble meant shooting. "The news of the Emancipation Act is leaking all over the place. Some of the troops in the north who haven't been disarmed yet are mutinying, and there are slave insurrections in a number of places."

"They think the Masters have forsaken them, and it's every slave for himself." He hadn't expected that to start so soon. "The announcement had better go out as quickly as possible. And I think we're going to have some trouble. You have information-taps into Count Erskyll's numerous staff? Use them as much as you can."

"You think he's going to try to sabotage this employment programme of yours, sir?"

"Oh, he won't think of it in those terms. He'll be preventing me from sabotaging the Emancipation. He doesn't want to wait three generations; he wants to free them at once. Everything has to be at once for six-month-old puppies, six-year-old children, and reformers of any age."

The announcement did not go out until nearly noon the next day. In terms comprehensible to any low-grade submoron, it was emphasized that all this meant was that slaves should henceforth be called freedmen, that they could have money just like Lords-Master, and that if they worked faithfully and obeyed orders they would be given everything they were now receiving. Ravney had been shuttling troops about, dealing with the sporadic outbreaks of disorder here and there: many of these had been put down, and the rest died out after the telecast explaining the situation.

In addition, some of Commander Douvrin's intelligence people had discovered that the only source of fissionables and radioactives for the planet was a complex of uranite mines, separation plants, refineries and reaction-plants on the smaller of Aditya's two continents, Austragonia. In spite of other urgent calls on his resources, Ravney landed troops to seize these, and a party of engineers followed them down from the *Empress Eulalie* to make an inspection.

At lunch, Count Erskyll was slightly less intransigent on the subject of the wage-employment proposals. No doubt some of his advisors had been telling him what would happen if any appreciable number of Aditya's labor-force stopped work suddenly, and the wave of uprisings that had broken out before any public announcement had been made puzzled [Pg 120] him. He was also concerned about finding a suitable building for a proconsular palace; the business of the Empire on Aditya could not be conducted long from shipboard.

Going down to the Citadel that afternoon, they found the chief-freedmen of the non-functional Chiefs of Management assembled in a large room on the fifth level down. There was a cluster of big tables and communication-screens and wired telephones in the middle, with smaller tables around them, at which freedmen in variously colored gowns sat. The ones at the central tables, a dozen and a half, all wore chief-slaves' white gowns.

Trevannion and Erskyll and Patrique Morvill and Lanze Degbrend joined these; subordinates guided the rest of the party—a couple of Ravney's officers and Erskyll's numerous staff of advisors and specialists—to distribute themselves with their opposite numbers in the Mastership. Everybody on the Adityan side seemed uneasy with these strange hermaphrodite creatures who were neither slaves nor Lords-Master.

"Well, gentlemen," Count Erskyll began, "I suppose you have been informed by your former Lords-Master of how relations between them and you will be in the future?"

"Oh, yes, Lord Proconsul," Khreggor Chmidd replied happily. "Everything will be just as before, except that the Lords-Master will be called Lords-Employer, and the slaves will be called freedmen, and any time they want to starve to death, they can leave their Employers if they wish."

Count Erskyll frowned. That wasn't just exactly what he had hoped Emancipation would mean to these people.

"Nobody seems to understand about this money thing, though," Zhorzh Khouzhik, Sesar Martwynn's chief-freedman said. "My Lord-Master—" He slapped himself across the mouth and said, "Lord-Employer!" five times, rapidly. "My Lord-*Employer* tried to explain it to me, but I don't think he understands very clearly, himself."

"None of them do."

The speaker was a small man with pale eyes and a mouth like a rat-trap; Yakoop Zhannar, chief-freedman to Ranal Valdry, the Provost-Marshal.

"Its really your idea, Prince Trevannion," Erskyll said. "Perhaps you can explain it."

"Oh, it's very simple. You see."

At least, it had seemed simple when he started. Labor was a commodity, which the worker sold and the employer purchased; a "fair wage" was one which enabled both to operate at a profit. Everybody knew that—except here on Aditya. On Aditya, a slave worked because he was a slave, and a Master provided for him because he was a Master, and that was all there was to it. But now, it seemed, there weren't any more Masters, and there weren't any more slaves.

"That's exactly it," he replied, when somebody said as much. "So now, if the slaves, I mean, freedmen, [Pg 121] want to eat, they have to work to earn money to buy food, and if the Employers want work done, they have to pay people to do it."

"Then why go to all the trouble about the money?" That was an elderly chief-freedman, Mykhyl Eschkhaffar, whose Lord-Employer, Oraze Borztall, was Manager of Public Works. "Before your ships came, the slaves worked for the Masters, and the Masters took care of the slaves, and everybody was content. Why not leave it like that?"

"Because the Galactic Emperor, who is the Lord-Master of these people, says that there must be no more slaves. Don't ask me why," Tchall Hozhet snapped at him. "I don't know, either. But they are here with ships and guns and soldiers; what can we do?"

"That's very close to it," he admitted. "But there is one thing you haven't considered. A slave only gets what his master gives him. But a free worker for pay gets money which he can spend for whatever he wants, and he can save money, and if he finds that he can make

freedmen."

Some of them were briefly puzzled; gradually, comprehension dawned. Obray, Count Erskyll, looked distressed; he seemed to be hoping, vainly, that they weren't thinking of what he suspected they were.

"How about the Mastership freedmen?" another asked. "We, here, will be paid by our Lords-Mas- . Lords-Employer. But everybody from the green robes down were provided for by the Mastership. Who will pay them, now?"

"Why, the Mastership, of course," Ridgerd Schferts said. "My Management—my Lord-Employer's, I mean—will issue the money to pay them."

"You may need a new printing-press," Lanze Degbrend said. "And an awful lot of paper."

"This planet will need currency acceptable in interstellar trade," Erskyll said.

Everybody looked blankly at him. He changed the subject:

"Mr. Chmidd, could you or Mr. Hozhet tell me what kind of a constitution the Mastership has?"

"You mean, like the paper you read in the Convocation?" Hozhet asked. "Oh, there is nothing at all like that. The former Lords-Master simply ruled."

No. They reigned. This servile *tammanihal*—another ancient Terran word, of uncertain origin—ruled.

"Well, how is the Mastership organized, then?" Erskyll persisted. "How did the Lord Nikkolon get to be Chairman of the Presidium, and the Lord Javasan to be Chief of Administration?"

That was very simple. The Convocation, consisting of the heads of all the Masterly families, actually small clans, numbered about twenty-five hundred. They elected the seven members of the Presidium, who drew lots for the Chairmanship. They served for life. Vacancies were filled by election on nomination of the surviving members. The Presidium appointed the Chiefs of Managements, who also served for life.

At least, it had stability. It was self-perpetuating.

"Does the Convocation make the laws?" Erskyll asked.

Hozhet was perplexed. "*Make* laws, Lord Proconsul? Oh, no. We have laws."

There were planets, here and there through the Empire, where an attitude like that would have been distinctly beneficial; planets with elective parliaments, every member of which felt himself obligated to get as many laws enacted during his term of office as possible.

"But this is dreadful; you *must* have a constitution!" Obray of Erskyll was shocked. "We will have to get one drawn up and adopted."

"We don't know anything about that at all," Khreggor Chmidd admitted. [Pg 123] "This is something new. You will have to help us."

"I certainly will, Mr. Chmidd. Suppose you form a committee—yourself, and Mr. Hozhet, and three or four others; select them among yourselves—and we can get together and talk over what will be needed. And another thing. We'll have to stop calling this the Mastership. There are no more Masters."

"The Employership?" Lanze Degbrend dead-panned.

Erskyll looked at him angrily. "This is something," he told the chief-freedmen, "that should not belong to the Employers alone. It should belong to everybody. Let us call it the Commonwealth. That means something everybody owns in common."

"Something everybody owns, nobody owns," Mykhyl Eschkhaffar objected.

"Oh, no, Mykhyl; it will belong to everybody," Khreggor Chmidd told him earnestly. "But somebody will have to take care of it for everybody. That," he added complacently, "will be you and me and the rest of us here."

"I believe," Yakoop Zhannar said, almost smiling, "that this freedom is going to be a wonderful thing. For us."

"I don't like it!" Mykhyl Eschkhaffar said stubbornly. "Too many new things, and too much changing names. We have to call slaves freedmen; we have to call Lords Master Lords-Employer; we have to call the Management of Servile Affairs the Management for Freedmen. Now we have to call the Mastership this new name, Commonwealth. And all

more money working for somebody else, he can quit his employer and get a better job."

"We hadn't thought of that," Khreggor Chmidd said. "A slave, even a chief-slave, was never allowed to have money of his own, and if he got hold of any, he couldn't spend it. But now." A glorious vista seemed to open in front of him. "And he can accumulate money. I don't suppose a common worker could, but [Pg 122] an upper slave. Especially a chief-slave." He slapped his mouth, and said, "Freedman!" five times.

"Yes, Khreggor." That was Ridgerd Schferts (Fedrig Daffysan; Fiscal Management). "I am sure we could all make quite a lot of money, now that we are these new things, for which we have no routine procedures and no directives. I wish these people had never heard of this planet."

"That makes at least two of us," Patrique Morvill said, *sotto voce*.

"Well, the planetary constitution can wait just a bit," Prince Trevannion suggested. "We have a great many items on the agenda which must be taken care of immediately. For instance, there's this thing about finding a proconsular palace."

A surprising amount of work had been done at the small tables where Erskyll's staff of political and economic and technological experts had been conferring with the subordinate upper-freedmen. It began coming out during the pre-dinner cocktails aboard the *Empress Eulalie*, continued through the meal, and was fully detailed during the formal debriefing session afterward.

Finding a suitable building for the Proconsular Palace would present difficulties. Real estate was not sold on Aditya, any more than slaves were. It was not only un-Masterly but illegal; estates were all entailed and the inalienable property of Masterly families. What was wanted was one of the isolated residential towers in Zeggensburg, far enough from the Citadel to avoid an appearance of too close supervision. The last thing anybody wanted was to establish the Proconsul in the Citadel itself. The [Pg 124] Management of Business of the Mastership, however, had promised to do something about it. That would mean, no doubt, that the *Empress Eulalie* would be hanging over Zeggensburg, serving as Proconsular Palace, for the next year or so.

The Servile Management, rechristened Freedmen's Management, would undertake to safeguard the rights of the newly emancipated slaves. There would be an Employment Code—Count Erskyll was invited to draw that up—and a force of investigators, and an enforcement agency, under Zhorzh Khouzhik.

One of Commander Douvrin's men, who had been at the Austragonia nuclear-industries establishment, was present and reported:

"Great Ghu, you ought to see that place! They've people working in places I wouldn't send an unshielded robot, and the hospital there is bulging with radiation-sickness cases. The equipment must have been brought here by the Space Vikings. What's left of it is the damnedest mess of goldbergery I ever saw. The whole thing ought to be shut down and completely rebuilt."

Erskyll wanted to know who owned it. The Mastership, he was told.

"That's right," one of his economics men agreed. "Management of Public Works." That would be Mykhyl Eschkhaffar, who had so bitterly objected to the new nomenclature. "If anybody needs fissionables for a power-reactor or radioactives for nuclear-electric conversion, his chief business slave gets what's needed. Furthermore, doesn't even have to sign for it."

"Don't they sell it for revenue?"

"Nifflheim, no! This government doesn't need revenue. This government supports itself by counterfeiting. When the Mastership needs money, they just have Ridgerd Schferts print up another batch. Like everybody else."

"Then the money simply isn't worth anything!" Erskyll was horrified, which was rapidly becoming his normal state.

"Who cares about money, Obray," he said. "Didn't you hear them, last evening? It's un-Masterly to bother about things like money. Of course, everybody owes everybody for everything, but it's all in the family."

"Well, something will have to be done about that!"

That was at least the tenth time he had said that, this evening.

It came practically as a thunderbolt when Khreggor Chmidd screened the ship the next afternoon to report that a Proconsular Palace had been found, and would be ready for occupancy in a day or so. The chief-freedmen of the Management of Business of the Mastership and of the Lord Chief Justiciar had found one, the Elegry Palace, which had been unoccupied except for what he described as a small caretaking staff for years, while two Masterly families disputed inheritance rights and slave lawyers quibbled endlessly before a slave judge. The chief freedman of the Lord Chief Justiciar had simply summoned judge and lawyers into his [Pg 125] office and ordered them to settle the suit at once. The settlement had consisted of paying both litigants the full value of the building; this came to fifty million stellies apiece. Arbitrarily, the stelly was assigned a value in Imperial crowns of a hundred for one. A million crowns was about what the building would be worth, with contents, on Odin. It would be paid for with a draft on the Imperial Exchequer.

"Well, you have some hard currency on the planet, now," he told Count Erskyll, while they were having a pre-dinner drink together that evening. "I hope it doesn't touch off an inflation, if the term is permissible when applied to Adityan currency."

Erskyll snapped his fingers. "Yes! And there's the money we've been spending for supplies. And when we start compensation payments. Excuse me for a moment."

He dashed off, his drink in his hand. After a long interval, he was back, carrying a fresh one he had gotten from a bartending robot en route.

"Well, that's taken care of," he said. "My fiscal man's getting in touch with Ridgerd Schferts; the Elegry heirs will be paid in Adityan stellies, and the Imperial crowns will be held in the Commonwealth Bank, or, better, banked in Asgard, to give Aditya some off-planet credit. And we'll do the same with our other expenditures, and with the slave-compensation. This is going to be wonderful; this planet needs everything in the way of industrial equipment; this is how they're going to get it."

"But, Obray; the compensations are owing to the individual Masters. They should be paid in crowns. You know as well as I do that this hundred-for-one rate is purely a local fiction. On the interstellar exchange, these stellies have a crown value of precisely zero-point-zero."

"You know what would happen if these ci-devant Masters got hold of Imperial crowns," Erskyll said. "They'd only squander them back again for useless imported luxuries. This planet needs a complete modernization, and this is the only way the money to pay for it can be gotten." He was gesturing excitedly with the almost-full glass in his hand; Prince Trevannion stepped back out of the way of the splash he anticipated. "I have no sympathy for these ci-devant Masters. They own every stick and stone and pinch of dust on this planet, as it is. Is that fair?"

"Possibly not. But neither is what you're proposing to do."

Obray, Count Erskyll, couldn't see that. He was proposing to secure the Greatest Good for the Greatest Number, and to Nifflheim with any minorities who happened to be in the way.

The Navy took over the Elegry Palace the next morning, ran up the Imperial Sun and Cogwheel flag, and began transmitting views of its interior up to the *Empress Eulalie*. It was considerably smaller than the Imperial Palace at Asgard on Odin, but room for room the furnishings were [Pg 126] rather more ornate and expensive. By the next afternoon, the counter-espionage team that had gone down reported the Masterly living quarters clear of pickups, microphones, and other apparatus of servile snooping, of which they had found many. The *Canopus* was recalled from her station over the northern end of the continent and began sending down the proconsulate furnishings stowed aboard, including several hundred domestic robots.

The skeleton caretaking staff Chmidd had mentioned proved to number five hundred.

"What are we going to do about them?" Erskyll wanted to know. "There's a limit to the upkeep allowance for a proconsulate, and we can't pay five hundred useless servants. The chief-freedman, and about a dozen assistants, and a few to operate the robots, when we train them, but five hundred.!"

"Let Zhorzh do it," Prince Trevannion suggested. "Isn't that what this Freedmen's Management is for; to find employment for emancipated slaves?

Just emancipate them and turn them over to Khouzhik."

Khouzhik promptly placed all of them on the payroll of his Management. Khouzhik was having his hands full. He had all his top mathematical experts, some of whom even understood the use of the slide-rule, trying to work up a scale of wages. Erskyll loaned him a few of his staff. None of the ideas any of them developed proved workable. Khouzhik had also organized a corps of investigators, and he was beginning to annex the private guard-companies of the Lords-ex-Master, whom he was organizing into a police force.

The nuclear works on Austragonia were closed down. Mykhyl Eschkhaffar ordered a programme of rationing and priorities to conserve the stock of plutonium and radioactive isotopes on hand, and he decided that henceforth nuclear-energy materials would be sold instead of furnished freely. He simply found out what the market quotations on Odin were, translated that into stellies, and adopted it. This was just a base price; there would have to be bribes for priority allocations, rakeoffs for the under-freedmen, and graft for the business-freedmen of the Lords-ex-Masters who bought the stuff. The latter were completely unconcerned; none of them even knew about it.

The Convocation adjourned until the next regular session, at the Midyear Feasts, an eight-day intercalary period which permitted dividing the 358-day Adityan year into ten months of thirty-five days each. Count Erskyll was satisfied to see them go. He was working on a constitution for the Commonwealth of Aditya, and was making very little progress with it.

"It's one of these elaborate check-and-balance things," Lanze Degbrend reported. "To begin with, it was the constitution of Aton, with an elective president substituted for a hereditary king. Of course, there are a lot of added gadgets; Atonian Radical Democrat stuff. Chmidd and Hozhet and [Pg 127] the other chief-slaves don't like it, either."

"Slap your mouth and say, 'Freedmen,' five times."

"Nuts," his subordinate retorted insubordinately. "I know a slave when I see one. A slave is a slave, with or without a gorget; if he doesn't wear it around his neck, he has it tattooed on his soul. It takes at least three generations to rub it off."

"I could wish that Count Erskyll." he began. "What else is our Proconsul doing?"

"Well, I'm afraid he's trying to set up some kind of a scheme for the complete nationalization of all farms, factories, transport facilities, and other means of production and distribution," Degbrend said.

"He's not going to try to do that himself, is he?" He was, he discovered, speaking sharply, and modified his tone. "He won't do it with Imperial authority, or with Imperial troops. Not as long as I'm here. And when we go back to Odin, I'll see to it that Vann Shatrak understands that."

"Oh, no. The Commonwealth of Aditya will do that," Degbrend said. "Chmidd and Hozhet and Yakoop Zhannar and Zhorzh Khouzhik and the rest of them, that is. He wants it done legitimately and legally. That means, he'll have to wait till the Midyear Feasts, when the Convocation assembles, and he can get his constitution enacted. If he can get it written by then."

Vann Shatrak sent two of the destroyers off to explore the moons of Aditya, of which there were two. The outer moon, Aditya-*Ba'*, was an irregular chunk of rock fifty miles in diameter, barely visible to the naked eye. The inner, Aditya-*Alif*, however, was an eight-hundred-mile sphere; it had once been the planetary ship-station and shipyard-base. It seemed to have been abandoned when the Adityan technology and economy had begun sagging under the weight of the slave system. Most of the installations remained, badly run down but repairable. Shatrak transferred as many of his technicians as he could spare to the *Mizar* and sent her to recondition the shipyard and render the underground city inhabitable again so that the satellite could be used as a base for his ships. He decided, then, to send the

Irma back to Odin with reports of the annexation of Aditya, a proposal that Aditya-*Alif* be made a permanent Imperial naval-base, and a request for more troops.

Prince Trevannion taped up his own reports, describing the general situation on the newly annexed planet, and doing nothing to minimize the problems facing its Proconsul.

"Count Erskyll" he finished, "is doing the best possible under circumstances from which I myself would feel inclined to shrink. If not carried to excess, perhaps youthful idealism is not without value in Empire statecraft. I understand that Commodore Shatrak, who is also coping with some very trying problems, is requesting troop reenforcements. I believe this request amply justified, and would recommend that they be [Pg 128] gotten here as speedily as possible.

"I understand that he is also recommending a permanent naval base on the larger of this planet's two satellites. This I also endorse unreservedly. It would have a most <u>salutary</u> effect on the local government. I would further recommend that Commodore Shatrak be placed in command of it, with suitable promotion, which he has long ago earned."

Erskyll was surprised that he was not himself returning to Odin on the destroyer, and evidently disturbed. He mentioned it during pre-dinner cocktails that evening.

"I know, my own work here is finished; was the moment the Convocation voted acknowledgment of Imperial rule. " Prince Trevannion replied. "I would like to stay on for the Midyear Feasts, though. The Convocation will vote on your constitution, and I would like to be able to report their action to the Prime Minister. How is it progressing, by the way?"

"Well, we have a rough draft. I don't care much for it, myself, but Citizen Hozhet and Citizen Chmidd and Citizen Zhannar and the others are most enthusiastic, and, after all, they are the ones who will have to operate under it."

The Masterly estates would be the representative units; from each, the

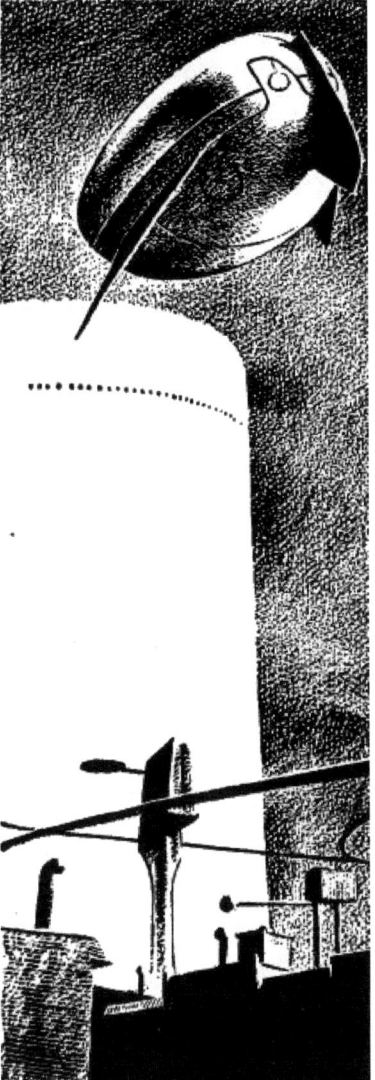

freedmen would elect representatives to regional elective councils, and these in turn would elect representatives to a central electoral council which would elect a Supreme People's Legislative Council. This would [Pg 129] not only function as the legislative body, but would also elect a Manager-in-Chief, who would appoint the Chiefs of Management, who, in turn, would appoint their own subordinates.

"I don't like it, myself," Erskyll said. "It's not democratic enough. There should be a direct vote by the people. Well," he grudged, "I suppose it will take a little time for them to learn democracy." This was the first time he had come out and admitted that. "There is to be a Constituent Convention in five years, to draw up a new constitution."

"How about the Convocation? You don't expect them to vote themselves out of existence, do you?"

"Oh, we're keeping the Convocation, in the present constitution, but they won't have any power. Five years from now, we'll be rid of them entirely. Look here; you're not going to work against this, are you? You won't advise these ci-devant Lords-Master to vote against it, when it comes up?"

"Certainly not. I think your constitution—Khreggor Chmidd's and Tchall Hozhet's, to be exact—will be nothing short of a political disaster, but it will insure some political stability, which is all that matters from the Imperial point of view. An Empire statesman must always guard against sympathizing with local factions and interests, and I can think of no planet on which I could be safer from any such temptation. If these Lords-Master want to vote their throats cut, and the slaves want to re-enslave themselves, they may all do so with my complete blessing."

If he had been at all given to dramatic gestures he would then have sent for water and washed his hands.

Metaphorically, he did so at that moment; thereafter his interest in Adityan affairs was that of a spectator at a boring and stupid show, watching only because there is nothing else to watch, and wishing that it had been possible to have returned to Odin on the *Irma*. The Prime Minister, however, was entitled to a full and impartial report, which he would scarcely get from Count Erskyll, on this new jewel in the Imperial Crown. To be able to furnish that, he would have to remain until the Midyear Feasts, when the Convocation would act on the new constitution. Whether the constitution was adopted or rejected was, in itself, unimportant; in either case, Aditya would have a government recognizable as such by the Empire, which was already recognizing some fairly unlikely-looking governments. In either case, too, Aditya would make nobody on any other planet any trouble. It wouldn't have, at least for a long time, even if it had been left unannexed, but no planet inhabited by Terro-humans could be trusted to remain permanently peaceful and isolated. There is a spark of aggressive ambition in every Terro-human people, no matter how debased, which may smoulder for centuries or even millennia and then burst, [Pg 130] fanned by some random wind, into flame. To shift the metaphor slightly, the Empire could afford to leave no unwatched pots around to boil over unexpectedly.

Occasionally, he did warn young Erskyll of the dangers of overwork and emotional over-involvement. Each time, the Proconsul would pour out some tale of bickering and rivalry among the chief-freedmen of the Managements. Citizen Khouzhik and Citizen Eschkhaffar—they were all calling each other Citizen, now—were contesting overlapping jurisdictions. Khouzhik wanted to change the name of his Management—he no longer bothered mentioning Sesar Martwynn—to Labor and Industry. To this, Mykhyl Eschkhaffar objected vehemently; any Industry that was going to be managed would be managed by his—Oraze Borztall was similarly left unmentioned—management of Public Works. And they were also feuding about the robotic and remote-controlled equipment that had been sent down from the *Empress Eulalie* to the Austragonia nuclear-power works.

Khouzhik was also in controversy with Yakoop Zhannar, who was already calling himself People's Provost-Marshal. Khouzhik had taken over all the private armed-guards on the Masterly farms and in the factories, and assimilated them into something he was calling the People's Labor Police, ostensibly to enforce the new Code of Employment Practice. Zhannar insisted that they should be under his Management; when Chmidd and Hozhet supported Khouzhik, he began clamoring for the return of the regular army to his control. Commodore Shatrak was more than glad to get rid of the Adityan army, and so was Pyairr Ravney, who was in immediate command of them. The Adityans didn't care one way or the other. Zhannar was delighted, and so were Chmidd and Hozhet. So, oddly, was Zhorzh Khouzhik. At the same time, the state of martial law proclaimed on the day of the landing was terminated.

The days slipped by. There were entertainments at the new Proconsular Palace for the Masterly residents of Zeggensburg, and Erskyll and his staff were entertained at Masterly palaces. The latter affairs pained Prince Trevannion excessively—hours on end of gorging uninspired cooking and guzzling too-sweet wine and watching ex-slave performers whose acts were either brutal or obscene and frequently both, and, more unforgivable, stupidly so. The Masterly conversation was simply stupid.

He borrowed a reconn-car from Ravney; he and Lanze Degbrend and, usually, one or another of Ravney's young officers, took long trips of exploration. They fished in mountain streams, and hunted the small deerlike game, and he found himself enjoying these excursions more than anything he had done in recent years; certainly anything since Aditya had come into the viewscreens of the *Empress Eulalie*. Once in a while, they claimed and received Masterly [Pg 131] hospitality at some large farming estate. They were always greeted with fulsome cordiality, and there was always surprise that persons of their rank and consequence should travel unaccompanied by a retinue of servants.

He found things the same wherever he stopped. None of the farms were producing more than a quarter of the potential yield per acre, and all depleting the soil outrageously. Ten slaves—he didn't bother to think of them as freedmen—doing the work of one, and a hundred of them taking all day to do what one robot would have done before noon. White-gowned chief-slaves lording it over green and orange gowned supervisors and clerks; overseers still carrying and frequently using whips and knouts and sandbag flails.

Once or twice, when a Masterly back was turned, he caught a look of murderous hatred flickering into the eyes of some upper-slave. Once or twice, when a Master thought his was turned, he caught the same look in Masterly eyes, directed at him or at Lanze.

The Midyear Feasts approached; each time he returned to the city he found more excitement as preparations went on. Mykhyl Eschkhaffar's Management of Public Works was giving top priority to redecorating the Convocation Chamber and the lounges and dining-rooms around it in which the Masters would relax during recesses. More and more Masterly families flocked in from outlying estates, with contragravity-flotillas and retinues of attendants, to be entertained at the city palaces. There were more and gaudier banquets and balls and entertainments. By the time the Feasts began, every Masterly man, woman and child would be in the city.

There were long columns of military contragravity coming in, too; troop-carriers and combat-vehicles. Yakoop Zhannar was bringing in all his newly recovered army, and Zhorzh Khouzhik his newly organized People's Labor Police. Vann Shatrak, who was now commanding his battle-line unit by screen from the Proconsular Palace, began fretting.

"I wish I hadn't been in such a hurry to terminate martial rule," he said, once. "And I wish Pyairr hadn't been so confoundedly efficient in retraining those troops. That may cost us a few extra casualties, before we're through."

Count Erskyll laughed at his worries.

"It's just this rivalry between Citizen Khouzhik and Citizen Zhannar," he said, "They're like a couple of ci-devant Lords-Master competing to give more extravagant feasts. Zhannar's going to hold a review of his troops, and of course, Khouzhik intends to hold a review of his police. That's all there is to it."

"Well, just the same, I wish some reenforcements would get here from Odin," Shatrak said.

Erskyll was busy, in the days before the Midyear Feasts, either conferring at the Citadel with the ex-slaves who were the functional heads [Pg 132] of the

Managements or at the Proconsular Palace with Hozhet and Chmidd and the chief-freedmen of the influential Convocation leaders and Presidium members. Everybody was extremely optimistic about the constitution.

He couldn't quite understand the optimism, himself.

"If I were one of these Lords-Master, I wouldn't even consider the thing," he told Erskyll. "I know, they're stupid, but I can't believe they're stupid enough to commit suicide, and that's what this amounts to."

"Yes, it does," Erskyll agreed, cheerfully. "As soon as they enact it, they'll be of no more consequence than the Assemblage of Peers on Aton; they'll have no voice in the operation of the Commonwealth, and none in the new constitution that will be drawn up five years from now. And that will be the end of them. All the big estates, and the factories and mines and contragravity-ship lines will be nationalized."

"And they'll have nothing at all, except a hamper-full of repudiated paper stellies," he finished. "That's what I mean. What makes you think they'll be willing to vote for that?"

"They don't know they're voting for it. They'll think they're voting to keep control of the Mastership. People like Olvir Nikkolon and Rovard Javasan and Ranal Valdry and Sesar Martwynn think they still own their chief-freedmen; they think Hozhet and Chmidd and Zhannar and Khouzhik will do exactly what they tell them. And they believe anything the Hozhets and Chmidds and Zhannars tell them. And every chief-freedman is telling his Lord-Employer that the only way they can keep control is by adopting the constitution; that they can control the elections on their estates, and hand-pick the People's Legislative Council. I tell you, Prince Trevannion, the constitution is as good as enacted."

Two days before the opening of the Convocation, the *Irma* came into radio-range, five light-hours away, and began transmitting in taped matter at sixty-speed. Erskyll's report and his own acknowledged; a routine "well done" for the successful annexation. Commendation for Shatrak's handling of the landing operation. Orders to take over Aditya-*Alif* and begin construction of a permanent naval base. Notification of promotion to base-admiral, and blank commission as line-commodore; that would be Patrique Morvill. And advice that one transport-cruiser, *Algol*, with an Army contragravity brigade aboard, and two engineering ships, would leave Odin for Aditya in fifteen days. The last two words erased much of the new base-admiral's pleasure.

"Fifteen days, great Ghu! And those tubs won't make near the speed of *Irma*, getting here. We'll be lucky to see them in twenty. And Beelzebub only knows what'll be going on here then."

Four times, the big screen failed to respond. They were all crowded [Pg 133] into one of the executive conference-rooms at the Proconsular Palace, the batteries of communication and recording equipment incongruously functional among the gold-encrusted luxury of the original Masterly furnishings. Shatrak swore.

"Andrey, I thought your people had planted those pickups where they couldn't be found," he said to Commander Douvrin.

"There is no such place, sir," the intelligence officer replied. "Just places where things are hard to find."

"Did you mention our pickups to Chmidd or Hozhet or any of the rest of the shaveheads?" Shatrak asked Erskyll.

"No. I didn't even know where they were. And it was the freedmen who found them," Erskyll said. "I don't know why they wouldn't want us looking in."

Lanze Degbrend, at the screen, twisted the dial again, and this time the screen flickered and cleared, and they were looking into the Convocation Chamber from the extreme rear, above the double doors. Far away, in front, Olvir Nikkolon was rising behind the gold and onyx bench, and from the speaker the call bell tolled slowly, and the buzz of over two thousand whispering voices diminished. Nikkolon began to speak:

"Seven and a half centuries ago, our fathers went forth from Morglay to plant upon this planet a new banner."

It was evidently a set speech, one he had recited year after year, and every Lord Chairman of the Presidium before him. The splendid traditions. The glories of the Masterly race. The all-conquering Space Vikings. The proud heritage of the Sword-Worlds. Lanze was fiddling with the control knobs, stepping up magnification and focusing on the speaker's head and shoulders. Then everybody laughed; Nikkolon had a small plug in one ear, with a fine wire running down to vanish under his collar. Degbrend brought back the full view of the Convocation Chamber.

Nikkolon went on and on. Vann Shatrak summoned a robot to furnish him with a cold beer and another cigar. Erskyll was drumming an impatient devil's tattoo with his fingernails on the gold-encrusted table in front of him. Lanze Degbrend began interpolating sarcastic comments. And finally, Pyairr Ravney, who came from Lugaluru, reverted to the idiom of his planet's favorite sport:

"Come on, come on; turn out the bull! What's the matter, is the gate stuck?"

If so, it came quickly unstuck, and the bull emerged, pawing and snorting.

"This year, other conquerors have come to Aditya, here to plant another banner, the Sun and Cogwheel of the Galactic Empire, and I blush to say it, we are as helpless against these conquerors as were the miserable barbarians and their wretched serfs whom our fathers conquered seven hundred and sixty-two years ago, whose descendants, until this [Pg 134] black day, had been our slaves."

He continued, his voice growing more impassioned and more belligerent. Count Erskyll fidgeted. This wasn't the way the Chmidd-Hozhet Constitution ought to be introduced.

"So, perforce, we accepted the sovereignty of this alien Empire. We are now the subjects of his Imperial Majesty, Rodrik III. We must govern Aditya subject to the Imperial Constitution." (Groans, boos; catcalls, if the Adityan equivalent of cats made noises like that.) "At one stroke, this Constitution has abolished our peculiar institution, upon which is based our entire social structure. This I know. But this same Imperial Constitution is a collapsium-strong shielding; let me call your attention to Article One, Section Two: *Every Empire planet shall be self-governed as to its own affairs, in the manner of its own choice and without interference.* Mark this well, for it is our guarantee that this government, of the Masters, by the Masters, and for the Masters, shall not perish from Aditya." (Prolonged cheering.)

"Now, these arrogant conquerors have overstepped their own supreme law. They have written for this Mastership a constitution, designed for the sole purpose of accomplishing the liquidation of the Masterly class and race. They have endeavored to force this planetary constitution upon us by threats of force, and by a shameful attempt to pervert the fidelity of our chief-slaves—I will not insult these loyal servitors with this disgusting new name, freedmen—so that we might, a second time, be tricked into voting assent to our own undoing. But in this, they have failed. Our chief-slaves have warned us of the trap concealed in this constitution written by the Proconsul, Count Erskyll. My faithful Tchall Hozhet has shown me all the pitfalls in this infamous document."

Obray, Count Erskyll, was staring in dismay at the screen. Then he began cursing blasphemously, the first time he had ever been heard to do so, and, as he was at least nominally a Pantheist, this meant blaspheming the entire infinite universe.

"The rats! The dirty treacherous rats! We came here to help them, and look; they've betrayed us.!" He lost his voice in a wheezing sob, and then asked: "Why did they do it? Do they want to go on being slaves?"

Perhaps they did. It wasn't for love of their Lords-Master; he was sure of that. Even from the beginning, they had found it impossible to disguise their contempt.

Then he saw Olvir Nikkolon stop short and thrust out his arm, pointing directly below the pickup, and as he watched, something green-gray, a remote-control contragravity lorry, [Pg 135] came floating into the field of the screen. One of the vehicles that had been sent down from the *Empress Eulalie* for use at the uranium mines. As it lifted and advanced toward the center of the room, the other Lords-Master were springing to their feet.

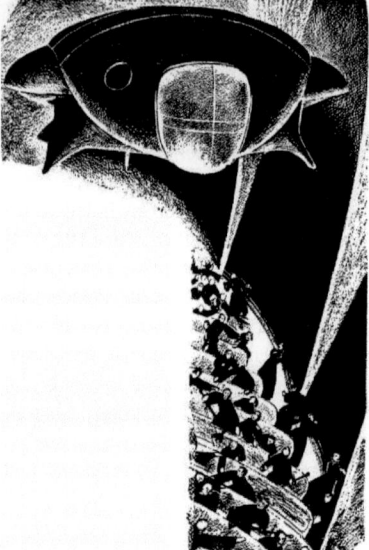

Vann Shatrak also sprang to his feet, reaching the controls of the screen and cutting the sound. He was just in time to save them from being, at least temporarily, deafened, for no sooner had he silenced the speaker than the lorry vanished in a flash that filled the entire room.

When the dazzle left their eyes, and the smoke and dust began to clear, they saw the Convocation Chamber in wreckage, showers of plaster and bits of plastiboard still falling from above. The gold and [Pg 136] onyx bench was broken in a number of places; the Chiefs of Management in front of it, and the Presidium above, had vanished. Among the benches lay black-clad bodies, a few still moving. Smoke rose from burning clothing. Admiral Shatrak put on the sound again; from the screen came screams and cries of pain and fright.

Then the doors on the two long sides opened, and red-brown uniforms appeared. The soldiers advanced into the Chamber, unslinging rifles and submachine guns. Unheeding the still falling plaster, they moved forward, firing as they came. A few of them slung their firearms and picked up Masterly dress swords, using them to finish the wounded among the benches. The screams grew fewer, and then stopped.

Count Erskyll sat frozen, staring white-faced and horror-sick into the screen. Some of the others had begun to recover and were babbling excitedly. Vann Shatrak was at a communication-screen, talking to Commodore Patrique Morvill, aboard the *Empress Eulalie*:

"All the Landing-Troops, and all the crewmen you can spare and arm. And every vehicle you have. This is only the start of it; there'll be a general massacre of Masters next. I don't doubt it's started already."

At another screen, Pyairr Ravney was saying, to the officer of the day of the Palace Guard: "No, there's no telling what they'll do next. Whatever it is, be ready for it ten minutes ago."

He stubbed out his cigarette and rose, and as he did, Erskyll came out of his daze and onto his feet.

"Commodore Shatrak! I mean, Admiral," he corrected himself. "We must re-impose martial rule. I wish I'd never talked you into terminating it. Look at that!" He pointed at the screen; big dump-lorries were already coming in the doors under the pickup, with a mob of gowned civil-service people crowding in under them. They and the soldiers began dragging bodies out from among the seats to be loaded and hauled away. "There's the planetary government, murdered to the last man!"

"I'm afraid we can't do anything like that," he said. "This seems to be a simple transfer of power by *coup-d'etat*; rather more extreme than usual, but normal political practice on this sort of planet. The Empire has no right to interfere."

Erskyll turned on him indignantly. "But it's mass murder!"

"It's an accomplished fact. Whoever ordered this, Citizen Chmidd and Citizen Hozhet and Citizen Zhannar and the rest of your good democratic citizens, are now the planetary government of Aditya. As long as they don't attack us, or repudiate the sovereignty of the Emperor, you'll have to recognize them as such."

"A bloody-handed gang of murderers; recognize them?"

"All governments have a little blood here and there on their hands; you've seen this by screen instead of reading about it in a history book, [Pg 137] but that shouldn't make any difference. And you've said, yourself, that the Masters would have to be eliminated. You've told Chmidd and Hozhet and the others that, repeatedly. Of course, you meant legally, by constitutional and democratic means, but that seemed just a bit too tedious to them. They had them all together in one room, where they could be eliminated easily, and . Lanze; see if you can get anything on the Citadel telecast."

Degbrend put on another communication-screen and fiddled for a moment. What came on was a view, from another angle, of the Convocation Chamber. A voice was saying:

". not one left alive. The People's Labor Police, acting on orders of People's Manager of Labor Zhorzh Khouzhik and People's Provost-Marshal Yakoop Zhannar, are now eliminating the rest of the ci-devant Masterly class, all of whom are here in Zeggensburg. The people are directed to cooperate; kill them all, men, women and children. We must allow none of these foul exploiters of the people live to see today's sun go down."

"You mean, we sit here while those animals butcher women and children?" Shatrak demanded, looking from the Proconsul to the Ministerial Secretary. "Well, by Ghu, I won't! If I have to face a court for it, all well and good, but."

"You won't, Admiral. I seem to recall, some years ago, a Commodore Hastings, who got a baronetcy for stopping a pogrom on Anath."

"And broadcast an announcement that any of the Masterly class may find asylum here at the Proconsular Palace. They're political fugitives; scores of precedents for that," Erskyll added.

Shatrak was back at the screen to the *Empress Eulalie*.

"Patrique, get a jam-beam focussed on that telecast station at the Citadel; get it off the air. Then broadcast on the same wavelength; announce that anybody claiming sanctuary at the Proconsular Palace will be taken in and protected. And start getting troops down, and all the spacemen you can spare."

At the same time, Ravney was saying, into his own screen:

"Plan Four. Variation H-3; this is a rescue operation. This is not, repeat, underscore, *not* an intervention in planetary government. You are to protect members of the Masterly class in danger from mob violence. That's anybody with hair on his head. Stay away from the Citadel; the ones there are all dead. Start with the four buildings closest to us, and get them cleared out. If the shaveheads give you any trouble, don't argue with them, just shoot them."

Erskyll, after his brief moment of decisiveness, was staring at the screen to the Convocation Chamber, where bodies were still being heaved into the lorries like black sacks of grain. Lanze Degbrend summoned a robot, had it pour a highball, and gave it to the Proconsul.

"Go ahead, Count Erskyll; drink it down. Medicinal," he was saying. [Pg 138] "Believe me you certainly need it."

Erskyll gulped it down. "I think I could use another, if you please," he said, handing the glass back to Lanze. "And a cigarette." After he had tasted his second drink and puffed on the cigarette, he said: "I was so proud. I thought they were learning democracy."

"We don't, any of us, have too much to be proud about," Degbrend told him. "They must have been planning and preparing this for a couple of months, and we never caught a whisper of it."

That was correct. They had deluded Erskyll into thinking that they were going to let the Masters vote themselves out of power and set up a representative government. They had deluded the Masters into believing that they were in favor of the *status quo*, and opposed to Erkyll's democratization and socialization. There must be only a few of them in the conspiracy. Chmidd and Hozhet and Zhannar and Khouzhik and Schferts and the rest of the Citadel chief-slave clique. Among them, they controlled all the armed force. The bickering and rivalries must have been part of the camouflage. He supposed that a few of the upper army commanders had been in on it, too.

A communication-screen began making noises. Somebody flipped the switch, and Khreggor Chmidd appeared in it. Erskyll swore softly, and went to face the screen-image of the elephantine ex-slave of the ex-Lord Master, the late Rovard Javasan.

"Citizen Proconsul; why is our telecast station, which is vitally needed to give information to the people, jammed off the air, and why are you broadcasting, on our wavelength, advice to the criminals of the ci-devant Masterly class to take refuge in your Proconsular Palace from the just vengeance of the outraged victims of their century-long exploitation?" he began. "This is a flagrant violation of the Imperial Constitution; our Emperor will not be pleased at this unjustified intervention in the affairs, and this interference with the planetary authority, of the People's Commonwealth of Aditya!"

Obray of Erskyll must have realized, for the first time, that he was still holding a highball glass in one hand and a cigarette in the other. He flung both of them away.

"If the Imperial troops we are sending into the city to rescue women and children in danger from your hoodlums meet with the least resistance, you won't be in a position to find out what his Majesty thinks about it, because Admiral Shatrak will have you and your accomplices shot in the Convocation Chamber, where you massacred the legitimate government of this planet," he barked.

So the real Obray, Count Erskyll, had at last emerged. All the liberalism and socialism and egalitarianism, all the Helping-Hand, Torch-of-Democracy, idealism, was merely a surface stucco applied at the university during the last six years. For twenty-four years before that, from [Pg 139] the day of his birth, he had been taught, by his parents, his nurse, his governess, his tutors, what it meant to be an Erskyll of Aton and a grandson of Errol, Duke of Yorvoy. As he watched Khreggor Chmidd in the screen, he grew angrier, if possible.

"Do you know what you bloodthirsty imbeciles have done?" he demanded. "You have just murdered, along with two thousand men, some five billion crowns, the money needed to finance all these fine modernization and industrialization plans. Or are you crazy enough to think that the Empire is going to indemnify you for being emancipated and pay that money over to you?"

"But, Citizen Proconsul."

"And don't call me Citizen Proconsul! I am a noble of the Galactic Empire, and on this pigpen of a planet I represent his Imperial Majesty. You will respect, and address, me accordingly."

Khreggor Chmidd no longer wore the gorget of servility, but, as Lanze Degbrend had once remarked, it was still tattooed on his soul. He gulped.

"Y-yes, Lord-Master Proconsul!"

They were together again in the big conference-room, which Vann Shatrak had been using, through the day, as an extemporised Battle-Control. They slumped wearily in chairs; they smoked and drank coffee; they anxiously looked from viewscreen to viewscreen, wondering when, and how soon, the trouble would break out again. It was dark, outside, now. Floodlights threw a white dazzle from the top of the Proconsular Palace and from the tops of the four buildings around it that Imperial troops had cleared and occupied, and from contragravity vehicles above. There was light and activity at the Citadel, and in the Servile City to the south-east; the rest of Zeggensburg was dark and quiet.

"I don't think we'll have any more trouble," Admiral Shatrak was saying. "They won't be fools enough to attack us here, and all the Masters are dead, except for the ones we're sheltering."

"How many did we save?" Count Erskyll asked.

Eight hundred odd, Shatrak told him. Erskyll caught his breath.

"So few! Why, there were almost twelve thousand of them in the city this morning."

"I'm surprised we saved so many," Lanze Degbrend said. He still wore combat coveralls, and a pistol-belt lay beside his chair. "Most of them were killed in the first hour."

And that had been before the landing-craft from the ships had gotten down, and there had only been seven hundred men and forty vehicles available. He had gone out with them, himself; it had been the first time he had worn battle-dress and helmet or carried a weapon except for sport in almost thirty years. It had been an ugly, bloody, business; one he wanted to forget as speedily as possible. There had been times, after seeing the mutilated bodies of Masterly women and children, when he had been forced to remind himself that he had come out to prevent, not [Pg 140] to participate in, a massacre. Some of Ravney's men hadn't even tried. Atrocity has a horrible facility for begetting atrocity.

"What'll we do with them?" Erskyll asked. "We can't turn them loose; they'd all be murdered in a matter of hours, and in any case, they'd have nowhere to go. The Commonwealth,"—he pronounced the name he had himself selected as though it were an obscenity—"has nationalized all the Masterly property."

That had been announced almost as soon as the Citadel telecast-station had been unjammed, and shortly thereafter they had begun encountering bodies of Yakoop Zhannar's soldiers and Zhorzh Khouzhik's police who had been sent out to stop looting and vandalism and occupy the Masterly palaces. There had been considerable shooting in the Servile City; evidently the ex-slaves had to be convinced that they must not pillage or destroy their places of employment.

"Evacuate them off-planet," Shatrak said. "As soon as *Algol* gets here, we'll load the lot of them onto *Mizar* or *Canopus* and haul them somewhere. Ghu only knows how they'll live, but."

"Oh, they won't be paupers, or public charges, Admiral," he said. "You know, there's an estimated five billion crowns in slave-compensation, and when I return to Odin I shall represent most strongly that these survivors be paid the whole sum. But I shall emphatically not recommend that they be resettled on Odin. They won't be at all grateful to us for today's business, and on Odin they could easily stir up some very adverse public sentiment."

"My resignation will answer any criticism of the Establishment the public may make," Erskyll began.

"Oh, rubbish; don't talk about resigning, Obray. You made a few mistakes here, though I can't think of a better planet in the Galaxy on which you could have made them. But no matter what you did or did not do, this would have happened eventually."

"You really think so?" Obray, Count Erskyll, was desperately anxious to be assured of that. "Perhaps if I hadn't been so insistent on this constitution."

"That wouldn't have made a particle of difference. We all made this inevitable simply by coming here. Before we came, it would have been impossible. No slave would have been able even to imagine a society without Lords-Master; you heard Chmidd and Hozhet, the first day, aboard the *Empress Eulalie*. A slave had to have a Master; he simply couldn't belong to nobody at all. And until you started talking socialization, nobody could have imagined property without a Masterly property-owning class. And a massacre like this would have been impossible to organize or execute. For one thing, it required an elaborate conspiratorial organization, and until we emancipated them, no slave would have dared trust any other slave; [Pg 141] every one would have betrayed any other to curry favor with his Lord-Master. We taught them that they didn't need Lords-Master, or Masterly favor, any more. And we presented them with a situation their established routines didn't cover, and forced them into doing some original thinking, which must have hurt like Nifflheim at first. And we retrained the army and handed it over to Yakoop Zhannar, and inspired Zhorzh Khouzhik to organize the Labor Police, and fundamentally, no government is anything but armed force. Really, Obray, I can't see that you can be blamed for anything but speeding up an inevitable process slightly."

"You think they'll see it that way at Asgard?"

"You mean the Prime Minister and His Majesty? That will be the way I shall present it to them. That was another reason I wanted to stay on here. I anticipated that you might want a credible witness to what was going to happen," he said. "Now, you'll be here for not more than five years before you're promoted elsewhere. Nobody remains longer than that on a first Proconsular appointment. Just keep your eyes and ears and, especially, your mind, open while you are here. You will learn many things undreamed-of by the political-science faculty at the University of Nefertiti."

"You said I made mistakes," Erskyll mentioned, ready to start learning immediately.

"Yes. I pointed one of them out to you some time ago: emotional involvement with local groups. You began sympathizing with the servile class here almost immediately. I don't think either of us learned anything about them that the other didn't, yet I found them despicable, one and all. Why did you think them worthy of your sympathy?"

"Why, because." For a moment, that was as far as he could get. His motivation had been thalamic rather than cortical and he was having trouble externalizing it verbally. "They were *slaves*. They were being exploited and oppressed."

"And, of course, their exploiters were a lot of heartless villains, so that made the slaves good and virtuous innocents. That was your real, fundamental, mistake. You know, Obray, the downtrodden and long-suffering proletariat aren't at all good or innocent or virtuous. They are just incompetent; they lack the abilities necessary for overt villainy. You saw, this afternoon, what they were capable of doing when they were given an opportunity. You know, it's quite all right to give the underdog a hand, but only one hand. Keep the other hand on your pistol—or he'll try to eat the one you gave him! As you may have noticed, today, when underdogs get up, they tend to turn out to be wolves."

"What do you think this Commonwealth will develop into, under Chmidd and Hozhet and Khouzhik and the rest?" Lanze Degbrend asked, to keep the lecture going.

"Oh, a slave-state, of course; look [Pg 142] who's running it, and whom it will govern. Not the kind of a slave-state we can do anything about," he hastened to add. "The Commonwealth will be very definite about recognizing that sapient beings cannot be property. But all the rest of the property will belong to the Commonwealth. Remember that remark of Chmidd's: 'It will belong to everybody, but somebody will have to take care of it for everybody. That will be you and me.'"

Erskyll frowned. "I remember that. I didn't like it, at the time. It sounded."

Out of character, for a good and virtuous proletarian; almost Masterly, in fact. He continued:

"The Commonwealth will be sole employer as well as sole property-owner, and anybody who wants to eat will have to work for the Commonwealth on the Commonwealth's terms. Chmidd's and Hozhet's and Khouzhik's, that is. If that isn't substitution of peonage for chattel slavery, I don't know what the word peonage means. But you'll do nothing to interfere. You will see to it that Aditya stays in the empire and adheres to the Constitution and makes no trouble for anybody off-planet. I fancy you won't find that too difficult. They'll be good, as long as you deny them the means to be anything else. And make sure that they continue to call you Lord-Master Proconsul."

Lecturing, he found, was dry work. He summoned a bartending robot:

"Ho, slave! Attend your Lord-Master!"

Then he had to use his ultraviolet pencil-light to bring it to him, and dial for the brandy-and-soda he wanted. As long as that was necessary, there really wasn't anything to worry about. But some of these days, they'd build robots that would anticipate orders, and robots to operate robots, and robots to supervise them, and.

No. It wouldn't quite come to that. A slave is a slave, but a robot is only a robot. As long as they stuck to robots, they were reasonably safe.

Transcriber's Notes & Errata

The original page numbers from the magazine have been retained.

The following typographical errors have been corrected.

Page	Error	Correction
65	Terrohuman	Terro-human
71	present;	present,
80	tessallated	tessellated
119	announcemnet	announcement
119	intransigeant	intransigent
127	tattoed	tattooed
128	salutory	salutary
132	constituion	constitution
134	belligerant	belligerent